D0442140

Praise for **Changeability**

'Europe's leading thinker on change.'

Business Strategy Review

'Change is constant and the ability to understand, instigate and lead change increasingly vital. Changeability tells you why and, most importantly, how. Vital reading for all those charged with leading change.'

Ron Whatford, Chief Experience Officer, Lloyds TSB

'There are many books on the topic of change but Michael Jarrett's very accessible exposition on how to successfully change an organisation is the first to confront head-on some of the biggest myths on this topic—myths such as the assumption that change is a planned process or the belief that it can be implemented in a series of linear steps. *Changeability* is full of examples and insights that will provoke, delight and educate. It will be a great addition to the library of every thoughtful manager.'

Costa Markides, Robert P Bauman Professor of Strategic Leadership, London Business School

'Change is a fact of life for every executive and in this immensely practical book Dr Jarrett uses his impressive research base to create a chart for executives to navigate the choppy waters of the corporate world. In *Changeability* he brings insights, diagnostic tools and a wealth of company examples to ensure that every company builds the internal capabilities that ensure they are ready for change, rather than a victim of change.'

Lynda Gratton, Professor of Management Practice at London Business School and author of *Hot Spots: why some teams, workplaces, and organisations buzz with energy – and others don't*

'Dr Michael Jarrett, a.k.a. the Professor of Change Management, presents in a clear and insightful way, through his years of research on the topic, and through thousands of interviews with those both leading corporate change as well as those affected by corporate changes, that there is in fact no prescribed formula for leading successful corporate changes. Instead his research has shown that each case is unique, and contends that understanding and responding to the external environment + building internal organisational capabilities + insightful leadership equals successful change. The book is vital for all industry leaders wishing to make their organisations change ready.'

Jeffrey S. Mack, CEO and President of Providence Washington Insurance Companies

'In *Changeability*, Michael Jarrett asks some very important questions about change, which are very relevant in these changing times. The book is based on extensive research which Michael uses, along with his own consulting experience to provide, clear ideas in a practical way.'

Roger Thomas, Partner, PwC

Changeability

Prentice Hall
FINANCIAL TIMES

In an increasingly competitive world, we believe it's
quality of thinking that gives you the edge – an idea
that opens new doors, a technique that solves a
problem, or an insight that simply makes sense of it all.
The more you know, the smarter and faster you can go.

That's why we work with the best minds in business and
finance to bring cutting-edge thinking and best learning
practice to a global market.

Under a range of leading imprints, including *Financial
Times Prentice Hall*, we create world-create print
publications and electronic products bringing our
readers knowledge, skills and understanding, which can
be applied whether studying or at work.

To find out about Pearson Education publications, or tell
us about the books you'd like to find, you can visit us at
www.pearsoned.co.uk

PEARSON
Education

Changeability

why some companies are ready for change –
and others aren't

Michael Jarrett

FT Prentice Hall
FINANCIAL TIMES

An imprint of **Pearson Education**

Harlow, England • London • New York • Boston • San Francisco • Toronto • Sydney • Singapore • Hong Kong
Tokyo • Seoul • Taipei • New Delhi • Cape Town • Madrid • Mexico City • Amsterdam • Munich • Paris • Milan

PEARSON EDUCATION LIMITED

Edinburgh Gate
Harlow CM20 2JE
Tel: +44 (0)1279 623623
Fax: +44 (0)1279 431059
Website: www.pearsoned.co.uk

First published in Great Britain in 2009

ISBN: 978-0-273-71289-3

British Library Cataloguing-in-Publication Data
A catalogue record for this book is available from the British Library

Library of Congress Cataloging-in-Publication Data
Jarrett, Michael.
  Changeability : why some companies are ready for change and others aren't / Michael
Jarrett.
      p. cm.
  Includes bibliographical references and index.
  ISBN 978-0-273-71289-3 (cased : alk. paper) 1. Organizational change. 2.
Organizational change--Management. I. Title.
  HD58.8.J37 2009
  658.4'06--dc22
                          2008043498

10 9 8 7 6 5 4 3 2 1
12 11 10 09 08

Typeset in 9.5pt Melior by 30
Printed and bound in Great Britain by Henry Ling Ltd, Dorchester

The publisher's policy is to use paper manufactured from sustainable forests.

About the author

Dr Michael Jarrett is one of Europe's leading experts on organisational change. He is an adjunct professor in organisational behaviour at London Business School and a founding partner of Ilyas Jarrett & Co, a research and management consulting firm that advises FTSE 100 companies on change management.

Michael was formerly managing director of the London office of Personnel Decisions International, a worldwide human-capital consultancy. Prior to that he was a director of the Alexander Corporation.

Michael's consultancy experience complements several academic posts. He has held faculty positions at Cranfield School of Management; taught at Bristol University and London University's Birkbeck College; and was a Research Fellow at Nottingham University. He was a staff consultant with the Tavistock Group Relations Conference and a policy adviser to central government at the National Council for Voluntary Organisations.

He has published articles on executive coaching and the role of the consultant in successful change, as well as 'The Seven Myths of Change Management' in *Business Strategy Review*.

To family and friends

The reason for being

It is not the strongest of the species that survives, nor the most intelligent, but the one most responsive to change.

Attributed to Charles Darwin

There is nothing more difficult to take in hand, more perilous to conduct, or more uncertain in its success, than to take the lead in the introduction of a new order of things.

Niccolò Machiavelli

Contents

part 4 **Leading change**

Publisher's acknowledgements

We are grateful to the following for permission to reproduce copyright material:

Figure 2.1 from 'Buy, buy, buy', *The Economist* ©The Economist Newspaper Limited, London (8 February 2007); Figure 2.2 from 'Solving GE's big problem', *The Economist* ©The Economist Newspaper Limited, London (24 October 2002); Figure 4.2 from 'Economic growth: The winning formula', *The Economist* ©The Economist Newspaper Limited, London (21 May 2008); Figure 6.1 from Proctor & Gamble, Connect + Develop[SM]; Figure 8.1 from 'Personal computers: There's life in the old dog yet', *The Economist* ©The Economist Newspaper Limited, London (30 August 2007); Figure 10.1 from 'Bitter pills: North American pharmaceutical firms', *The Economist* ©The Economist Newspaper Limited, London (28 June 2007) Figure 10.2 from Thomson Reuters Datastream.

In some instances we have been unable to trace the owners of copyright material and we would appreciate any information that would enable us to do so.

Author's acknowledgements

THERE ARE SO MANY PEOPLE who have contributed to this book. Some did so intentionally and others through wistful conversations that sparked an otherwise latent thought.

Being at London Business School provides a network of information, ideas and inspiration. There are a number of colleagues who have supported me in bringing my ideas to birth. These particularly include Lynda Gratton and Costas Markiadis who offered valuable comments, encouragement and the generosity of their time and experience. Others have provided intellectual encouragement and these include Nigel Nicholson, Madan Pillutla and Randall Peterson.

There are many who have also contributed to the research behind the book. My colleague and friend Lee White has travelled the longest distance and has been an enormous source of energy, ideas and friendly critique. Stefan Thau and Henry Moon reviewed the statistics and Kyle Ingram and Navaid Ilyas helped in completing background research and case material. It also goes without saying that building on the shoulders of other researchers provides strong conceptual and empirical roots.

Several of the ideas were tested in the real world of consulting with clients and teaching in the classroom at London Business School. In particular, I would like to thank Richard Ward of Lloyds, Allen Leighton of Royal Mail, Anne Mette Barfod of Copenhagen Re, Ron Whatford of Lloyds TSB, Jacques Agrain and Cheryl Mayo of Swiss Re and Jeff Mack of Providence Washington Solutions along with Arun Singh of Google and many others who have contributed their insights and access to their organisation so we can learn more. Executives and students have also helped. Participants span a wide range of programmes for Barclays Bank, as well as open programmes at London Business School such as the Accelerated Development

Programme and the Senior Executive Programme. Students on the managing change elective and consulting elective have all helped. The thinking and application of ideas have also been sharpened through consulting engagements with my colleagues at Ilyas Jarrett, an independent research and consulting firm.

The world of the internet has also been a wizard. Sources and search engines such as *The Economist*, *Financial Times*, *Guardian* and other tools make the world of writing and checking facts a whole lot easier than when I was an undergraduate. In those days you had to go down into the stacks in the basement. Now you can check papers and information from the comfort of your study. Thank you, Tim Berners-Lee, the father of the world wide web.

I would also like to thank several readers of earlier drafts. Mary Akimoto, Rohina Ilyas and Andrew Scott as well as anonymous referees, all contributed to making this book clearer. The editorial team has been great. Liz Gooster, Des Dearlove and Stuart Crainer have provided the helpful steer that brought thoughts to life. I would also like to say thank you to Richard Stagg, who originally encouraged and supported the ideas of the book. I still have his original exchange of emails.

I would also like to thank Jayna Patel, Remi Fasanya and Karen Lacey who helped co-ordinate the different parts of the final manuscript.

Finally, I want to thank my family and friends who have put up with me spending hours in my study and time away. I'd like to give a big thank you to my children and wife.

It goes without saying that all mistakes are my own.

Preface: What do we mean by change and changeability?

Change means different things to different people. To the CEO, it may mean increasing profits, cutting costs or saving the business; to you or me, it may mean no more and no less than keeping or losing our job. That is why change is so profoundly unsettling. And the less control we have over the change, the more unsettling it tends to be.

Of course, not every organisational change is job-threatening. A dictionary definition of *change* is 'the act or an instance of making or becoming different; an alteration or modification'. This suggests – entirely accurately – that change comes in many shapes and sizes.

Indeed, the word *change* is used to cover a multitude of situations: everything from the mundane – putting on a pair of clean socks – to the profound, physiological alterations that occur during midlife. Organisational change, too, comes in different degrees and guises. I distinguish between four main types:

First, there is *temporary change*. It looks as if things are going to change, but the organisation reverts to type and nothing happens. Any initiative quickly peters out, often after creating false hope. The organisation is simply not ready for change.

How often have you seen the Big Bang approach to change, in which considerable time and effort is placed on announcing the forthcoming strategic agenda and how everyone will gain from the benefits – yet life remains the same? In these instances, the illusion of change substitutes for any reality. More damp squib than big bang. Employees feel disappointed and let down. It's something they have heard before. Soon lethargy and mistrust seep in and turn to chronic cynicism. The situation becomes toxic; only radical surgery can fix it.

Second, there is *incremental* or *process change*. This sort of change aims to provide some small improvements. It is easy and quick to implement, and you get quick returns. The risk of failure is low, but so are returns in terms of benefits. Incremental change means operating within strict controls to gain efficiencies from your company's system of organisation. Fine-tuning a winning formula usually characterises this type of change.

You know the sort of thing. In one study, for example, a call centre in Sunderland increased its productivity by 20 per cent by introducing simple measures that included staff training and the implementation of new software. Incremental changes and training in another company produced an extra $110.25 per month per sales agent, for a 500-seat call centre. Over a year, that is worth an estimated $661,500 in sales. This sort of incremental change is useful – worth having, certainly – but unlikely to transform the organisation's competitive position.[1]

The third form of change is *organisational restructuring*. Here, the change focuses on fundamental systems, structures and relationships within the business. The introduction of a new sales force to increase market penetration is a typical example. These changes can take up to a year to embed, depending on the scale. The risks increase, but so do the rewards.

Supermarkets adding an online distribution channel is an example of this form of change. The UK retail chain Tesco was among the first to move to an internet strategy on a large scale in the retail grocery market. In the initial phase it meant restructuring the company's distribution channels to get the best returns from its existing assets. The company tended to pick groceries from existing stores that acted as local hubs. It had to implement new structures and systems to meet the needs of its new online customers.

Finally, there are *transformational and cultural-change programmes* that aim to redefine the organisation's strategic direction, cultural assumptions and identity. Examples include IBM moving from hardware to software, Polaroid moving from film to digital photography, and BT moving from telecoms to becoming an internet

1 Mohamed, Arif (2005) *Computer Weekly*, 20 September, p.22; and *CED* (2005) June, 31, 6, p.18.

provider. Larger-scale change initiatives such as these yield greater returns, but the risks – and stakes – are also much higher. The core of these companies get restructured, revitalised and renewed.

Nissan was a car company in deep trouble at the beginning of the 2000s. It had $17 billion of debt and looked like another wreck on the rocks of change. Carlos Ghosn took the helm – and completely transformed it. Within four years, Nissan was one of the world's most profitable car makers. The cultural and strategic changes Ghosn implemented marked a transformational change. He took a deep cut at the heart of the organisation's DNA and reinvented it to meet the challenges of the fiercely competitive and cost-conscious car industry. The car industry continues to throw up challenges for manufacturers. Only those prepared to change will survive. Nissan has a fighting chance because of the changes it has already made: others will be left behind.

Organisations want to avoid temporary change, an issue that surfaces as a theme when we look at organisational inertia. Incremental change can generate value under the right conditions. This sort of change tends to be more successful, but the value is small. It is really about exploiting the assets you already have.

Restructuring and transformational change are of greater interest. These hold the allure of greater value but, equally, the dangers of greater risk. It is with these two types of change where most of the problems lie – as well as most of the personal, organisational and financial rewards.

The unpalatable truth is that profound organisational change – change involving restructuring and transformation – is hard. The bigger the intended change, the bigger the prize and the harder the fall if it goes wrong. Research repeatedly suggests that managers attempting large-scale change are more likely to fail than succeed.

In my experience, one of the things that goes wrong with change programmes – again and again – is that organisations and leaders fail to reconcile or even understand their internal capabilities and the complexity of their external worlds. They either respond to a change in the external environment without thinking of the internal repercussions, or attempt to force through changes that make sense internally but no longer fit the context.

It doesn't have to be this way. This book lays out a tried and tested approach to change that can reap big rewards while minimising risks. It translates the complexities of change into clear actions that draw upon the latest research and practical consulting experience. It also has a huge data pool of executive responses so that you can get a realistic benchmark on your personal and organisational abilities. It provides strategies for change that lead to success and stop you becoming another statistic of failure. It shows you how to increase your *changeability*. Interested? Read on.

Michael Jarrett
London, 2008

The challenge of change

Strategic analysis is important. I'm not denying it. But *implementation* is the difference between success and failure. The best-laid plans of CEOs and managers come to nothing unless they are able to make change happen. The great managerial challenge lies not in understanding what needs to change (although that is a vital starting point) but in making it happen. It's all down to changeability.

The core of change management is executing successful organisational routines and deploying resources to fit strategic demands and create long-term growth. That is what this book is all about. Part 1 provides an overview of the challenge and the results of our research on the solution. It identifies the key factors that make a difference and answers the thorny question of why change so often fails.

Making change work

One of my most memorable holidays was with my family at Salcombe, in Devon in the south-west of England. Salcombe is famous for its sailing, and as I am a keen sailor, the prospect of taking the family out in my Wayfarer dinghy was a major attraction. We had a couple of days left, and I was desperate to get out onto the water before returning to our hectic London life. But this being an English summer the weather did not look good. There was a medium-force wind, the sea looked choppy and dark clouds hung over the horizon. We'd be lucky to get a few minutes sailing in. But my two sons – aged 11 and 13 – were ready and mostly willing, so we decided to try it.

The first attempt out of the sheltered bay of South Sands lasted about 10 minutes. My two sons were experienced hands on the jib (the small front) sail and we got off to a good start, but the worsening weather and unsheltered waters made for a difficult ride. Sea spray was constantly splashing our faces, and the bitter wind meant cold hands. They were having a miserable time, so I quickly turned our dinghy around and headed for the shore.

Somewhat disappointed, back on dry land I canvassed some of our friends to see if they were willing but there were no takers. Then a small voice said: 'I'll come.' It was my 10-year-old daughter. She was competent and had sailing experience, but I thought it probably wasn't a good idea. 'Not this time,' I said. 'I don't think you'd enjoy it.' 'No,' she said. 'I really want to do it, Dad. It'll be fun.'

Five minutes and a great deal of persistence later, I was pushing the boat into the waves and she was helming us out into the bay. By now the weather looked worse. My thought was that we'd do a few minutes in the shelter of the bay and then return.

Once we were away from the shore, the wind was brisk. By now my daughter was at the jib sheet and I was helming. We could see the rain coming in even before it hit us. Another couple of minutes, I decided, and then we would go back.

The wind meant we had plenty of power in the main sail, and we were cutting through the bay with considerable speed for such a large dinghy. We quickly had stability and before long hit the open water. We could see the rolling waves of the sea and braced for the first encounter. We tacked and turned quickly and were catapulted at 45 degrees in the other direction. My daughter gave a shriek – not of fear but of joy – as the waves whirled around us and led us off on another encounter. We darted for another 30 metres and tacked again. Again, sounds of glee and joy met the turn. The minutes went by, but we didn't turn around. I reconsidered.

We quickly established a crooked loop between the open water and the easy safety of the bay and went on, turn after turn, with more and more fun and enjoyment as the sense of adventure took over and caution, fear and anxiety receded. My daughter's reaction had a profound effect on me. We were not really in any danger, and there were always rescue boats within reach already on the water. No, it was her sense of adventure and enjoyment of the moment. It seemed to provide liberation for us both. The clouds magically seemed to hang back. We ended up staying on the water for the next 45 minutes.

Our friends commented that when we came back to shore, we strode back like victorious gladiators: heads high, chests out and swaggering. Our faces glowed with excitement, and we both felt a real sense of achievement. It was not what I had expected when we set out. It was not what I had planned. That day, I was given the gift of surprise.

Learning to change

I learned something from that experience – something real and life-enhancing. Change is a fact of life, often wonderful and sometimes worrying. Changes can be large- or small-scale, but they are often unplanned. Change is like death and taxes: inevitable. But that doesn't mean that it can't be exciting, invigorating and incredibly uplifting.

The point is that although change is inevitable, we have a choice about the way we respond. Out on that bay in Devon, I was a victim of change but also, as a responsible parent, an active agent of change – as most of us are. We have to make choices when confronted by change. We can decide to embrace it or resist it.

My best-laid plans were surprisingly overtaken by unplanned events. The day I had planned did not materialise, but a special day with my daughter did – only because I responded positively to the change.

Sailing is actually a very good metaphor for change, one I often use in my classroom. What I like best about it is that when a good sailor considers a manoeuvre, he or she takes account of many factors. These include internal capabilities such as the vessel's speed and seaworthiness and the crew's level of discipline and training. But it also includes external conditions such as rocks, difficult currents and weather. Just before he or she tacks in one direction or the other, the skipper calls out, 'Ready about!' It is a warning to the crew that they are about to make a change.

It is a poor skipper who tries to execute a manoeuvre that is either beyond the ability of the boat or crew, or who places their safety in jeopardy due to the prevailing conditions.

That doesn't mean that the skipper does not have to change the position of the boat – after all, change is inevitable. It just means that he or she must adopt the appropriate strategy. The same principles apply whether you are helming a dinghy, a yacht or a multinational corporation.

The universal change

Change happens, to me, to you and to the organisations we work for and encounter in our daily lives. Change is a fact of life – both personal and professional. Understanding change has been my passion for over a decade. I have become fascinated by how people and organisations deal with – and often avoid – change. Some people and organisations are much better than others at dealing with change.

The questions I continually ask are:

▌ Why are some companies able to transform themselves, while others fail?

▌ Why do some leaders inspire their people to try new things, while others encounter only cynicism?

▌ Why do some leaders succeed in making change a reality, while others never seem to reach a destination?

The answers to these questions underpin this book. The people I have talked to along the way have also convinced me that change – whether at work or in our private lives – need not be an unpleasant or demoralising experience. Change can and should be in our individual interests as well as our organisations'. But it will be only if we are properly prepared for it.

Anyone who has ever been involved with organisational change knows how hard it is to achieve. No matter how determined you are, or how sure you are that it is the right thing to do, galvanising people around you to make it happen is a huge challenge.

Yet, for a growing number of us, the ability to manage change will make or break our careers. Face it: in the modern world, change is what managers *do*. Managing successful change can be the difference between promotion and getting fired. It is as simple and challenging – and as brutal – as that.

Whether you are the CEO of an ailing multinational brought in to pull off a corporate turnaround in a recession, a middle manager charged with restructuring your department to improve efficiency, or a new recruit cutting your managerial teeth on your first change project, you have to get it right.

Teaching at London Business School, I find that the detailed questions on the minds of managers tend to be similar. Why change? What type of change should we adopt? How do you get buy in, deal with resistance and make it happen? This book addresses these important practical questions as well.

The vital spark

So what makes the difference between successful and unsuccessful change? That is the question that my research has addressed for the past 10 years. My interest goes all the way back to my doctoral work in the early 1990s. Since then, I have taught and interviewed literally thousands of executives at all levels, consulted to global companies, and for the past five years surveyed a further 5,000 executives from more than 250 companies around the world. I have spoken to people from pharmaceuticals to financial services, from strategy to human resources. I have interviewed real managers, people at the coal face of change. Some of them, it's true, were corporate leaders, CEOs and managing directors, but many more were ordinary managers who have achieved extraordinary results because they understand how change really works. I believe the result is among the most diverse databases of its kind.

And what have I discovered from all that research? What is my big conclusion? It may not be the answer you want to hear. But here goes anyway.

The result of all my labours is to confirm what I already suspected: there is no simple recipe for organisational transformation. There is no silver-bullet strategy, no simple one way that will deliver change. Sorry, but that's how it is. But you already knew that. Like me, you intuitively know this is the case. Deep down, we all understand that change is not a one-dimensional process.

That explains why the simple step-process models of change don't work. If making change happen were as easy as following simple universal rules, 70 per cent of change programmes wouldn't fail, as they do now. No matter how much we wish that there were one tool – a universal hammer that could crack any nut – we know the real world isn't like that.

That's the bad news. Now for the good: it is not about luck either. Managers who achieve successful change do something different. They may not consciously know they are doing it, but they are doing it all the same. They are selecting an appropriate change strategy – one that matches their internal capabilities and their external challenges.

My research shows that the best predictor of the success or failure of organisational change is *changeability.* I see this as the sum of leadership, internal routines and organisational capabilities that make companies fit and ready for change.

What do I mean by readiness for change? Readiness for change applies at the philosophical level – being open to and prepared to embrace change – but it also applies at the practical level. Readiness applies to those organisations that have developed a set of core dynamic and internal capabilities that allow them to adapt when faced by external demands. Basically, successful change is a function of how well an organisation's internal capabilities – its management capacity, culture, processes, resources and people – match the requirements of its external environment, the marketplace.

The secret to the management of change is not only what happens on the outside – it is how we respond on the inside, as leaders and as organisations. This is the essential lesson of managing change. To make change stick, we must have organisational readiness. To repeat Pasteur's words, 'Chance favours the prepared mind.' It is also true that organisations with high levels of readiness favour change.

So if you want to succeed at introducing change, you need to understand that different situations demand different strategies for change. Simply put:

Internal capabilities + External environment + Leadership = CHANGEABILITY

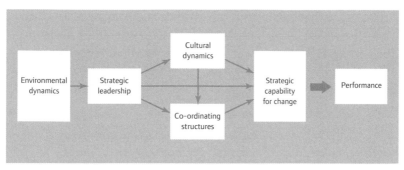

FIGURE 1.1 The overall model

The overall model (Figure 1.1) charts the ideas in the book. The internal capabilities that set your changeability are seen in strategic leadership, the culture and the structure of the organisation. The environmental dynamics often create the drivers for change and how you respond with change strategies affects organisational performance.

The rest of Part 1 of the book addresses three questions:

1 Why do so many change initiatives fail?

2 What is the difference between organisations that are successful in effecting change and those that are not?

3 How can you tell whether you are ready to change and make change stick?

In Part 2 of the book, we look more deeply at each side of the equation. It will provide you with answers to the burning questions of: How do I know if my company has changeability? What are the consequences if I do not? Will my company be more successful? How do I go about increasing the odds of success?

Each chapter deals with a crucial question:

▌ Why does the organisation's environment matter?

▌ Does top leadership make a difference?

▌ How do you get people on board?

▌ How do you structure an organisation for change?

In Part 3, I look at the interaction between an organisation's internal change capabilities (organisational readiness) and its external environment. My research has identified four zones or types of environment. The factors discussed in Part 2 determine which of the four an organisation (or business unit or department) is in and how best to achieve the required change.

In Part 4, these elements come together by looking at personal change leadership and the importance of self-regulation, self-awareness and commitment on behalf of the advocates of change. It provides an opportunity for self-reflection and to work on your own personal readiness.

At the heart of the book is a diagnostic test[1] to benchmark your organisation against others in terms of your changeability and to assess your relative strengths and weaknesses. That diagnosis allows you to select the appropriate strategy, tools, methods and techniques to develop change strategies customised for your company. There are four main groups of strategies, depending upon your situation, so choose the one that's right for you and open the door to accelerated and sustainable change.

In sum: this book provides a chart for leaders of change to navigate through choppy waters and find their way around the hidden rocks to their intended destination. The journey, however, requires preparation, and the following chapters help you do just that.

The core of *Changeability* explains how to make change stick in practice.

Summary

▌ Change is a feature of life, bringing both pain and unexpected pleasures.

▌ One of the secrets to managing change lies in how we respond, both as leaders and individuals.

[1] The Strategic Capability inventory (SCi™) is the research questionnaire that was used to assess company capabilities. A shortened version is provided in Appendix 2 and 3. The full version is available for your company to get a true sense of its bench strength at www.ilyasjarrett.com.

▌ A major difference between those companies that succeed in change and those that do not is their 'changeability'. This reflects their attitude and the internal core and dynamic capabilities that help them adapt to changes in the external environment.

▌ Change strategies that take account of the internal and external conditions are more likely to succeed. They provide choice and improve performance.

The hard truths

The difference between stumbling blocks and stepping stones is how you use them.

Unknown

How does a leader successfully implement far-reaching changes across an organisation in the face of external dramatic demands? This was a question I asked Richard Ward, who served as CEO of the International Petroleum Exchange (IPE). Richard started his career as a scientist and academic. His razor-sharp thinking meant he quickly grasped the complexities and rhythm of the business world and was able to spot trends. So he was fully prepared for what happened when he announced, in spring 2005, that the IPE oil exchange would be changing from 'open outcry' on the floor of the exchange to electronic trading using terminals.

The change – a seemingly inevitable update given technological advances and increasingly global finance – met with unexpectedly fierce opposition. At one point, Richard found himself physically threatened, seized by the throat and pinned to the wall, such was the high level of emotions that ran at the time. At the other end of the burly hands was one of the traders from the floor of the exchange. He was six feet tall and all he could see was the end of an era.

The trader had worked at the exchange boy and man. He was good at his job and made outstanding money. It was his life. The 'open outcry' floor represented years of tradition and ritual – men in strangely coloured coats, shouting and accepting bids in a cacophony of yells and excitement. It was a true reflection of Adam Smith's 'invisible hand' of capitalism: information was widely known by all; exchange was at a fair price; there were lots of buyers and sellers. It was a perfect market driven by the animal spirits of supply and demand. Now it was all going to change with electronic trading. Why replace a clear system for one that was, granted, even more transparent, quicker and easier to do business, and that allowed instant access to aggregate data? What were they thinking? It is easy for us as readers to see the benefits. But for the recipients of change it can be difficult to see the advantages. They can be overwhelmed by the downsides.

Indeed, many of the traders on the floor rejected the Big Brother changes and regarded the switch to electronic trading as heresy. They saw no advantages in the new system. It would take the heart and soul out of the process, they argued. It meant the end of an era. They announced their intention to fight the change to the bitter end, and they did.

Let's be clear. The idea of moving to electronic trading was a good strategic decision. The trends and moves at other major markets, such as the Chicago Mercantile Exchange, meant that the IPE needed to respond to the times. So, it was a sensible strategy, but waiting in the wings was the potential for it to unravel into chaos and despair.

Given the patent need for change and the internal opposition, how did Richard Ward and his team make the transition work? Clearly, they had a long haul. Along the way, he successfully helped to navigate two strands to the change strategy. The first was the external environment. Constant vigilance and extensive networks provided him and his small change team with the information and resources they needed to structure the right deal within the current climate of hostile competition, a drive for cost saving and the onslaught of technology across the world's major bourses. Operating and negotiating with a network of agents, brokers and stakeholders maintained good relationships in the market.

Managing the internal capability was also part of his secret. The need for change was properly communicated and understood, thus addressing initial major concerns. An example of the change team's ingenuity was that they allowed traders to also use the terminals as game consoles. It helped the transition. Before long the advantages became apparent and the downsides mitigated. They closed the trading floor, provided more access points through computer terminals to increase the transparency and speed of trading, reduced errors and provided a secure base for the market. Richard involved internal stakeholders and eventually managed to find the critical mass to make the changes work.

The changes took place in a hostile environment, but the top team managed the external and internal worlds of the organisation – and produced a successful outcome. The secret to their success: devising a change strategy that aligned and developed their internal capability with the pressures of the external demands.

Richard is not alone. He was smart enough to react and correct things, but his experience emphasises the point that most strategies fail not because of poor strategic analysis but because of poor implementation.

Is change really so hard?

Consider mergers and acquisitions. The glittering prize of M&As continues to be irresistibly alluring and offers a great opportunity for companies to grow. Inevitably, a merger or acquisition involves change on a massive scale. This fact has hardly dented dealmakers' enthusiasm: according to one survey, cross-border M&As have markedly increased in the past few years, particularly in Europe.[1] In 2006, the value of European M&As actually topped those in America, at $1.59 trillion. Though it is unlikely that this trend can continue, M&As will certainly remain a notable feature of the business world for years to come. And yet, they come with so much baggage...

A PricewaterhouseCoopers study found that two-thirds of buyers' stock dropped appreciably on announcement of a major acquisition,

[1] 'Buy, buy, buy', *The Economist*, 8 February 2007.

and that more than one-third of these companies still lagged behind the levels of peer companies a year later. To cite one of countless examples, a year after Daimler-Benz took over Chrysler in 1998, the value of the combined company had fallen below pre-merger levels (see Figure 2.1).

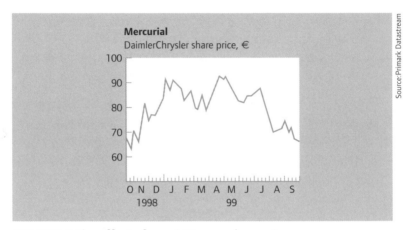

FIGURE 2.1 The effect of acquisition on share price

Indeed, study after study suggests that less than one in three mergers create the surplus value intended. These odds are not for the fainthearted. You'd be better off putting your money either under the mattress or, if you are the betting type, on a horse!

Large-scale changes are also a risk

It isn't just change initiatives created by M&As that go awry. Other changes hit the corporate buffers. A comprehensive study of organisational change across Europe highlighted that while the benefits of transformational and large-scale change were attractive, the realisation of the benefits is more elusive. The researchers estimated that less than 1 in 20 companies were able to gain the value they intended from large-scale change.[2]

[2] Whittington, R., Pettigrew, A., Peck, S., Fenton, E. and Conyon, M. (1999) 'Change and Complementarities in the New Competitive Landscape: A European Panel Study, 1992–1996', *Organization Science*, 10, 5, pp.583–600.

On the nature of this type of change, the research findings err on the side of caution. In a 1997 paper, Princeton University sociologist Martin Ruef concluded that most organisations are unable to match the structural changes in their competitive environments owing to relative structural inertia.[3] Others argue that less than 30 per cent are able to make such order of change stick.[4]

However, empirical findings suggest that transformational and large-scale changes tend to reap better value if successful.[5]

One study of 59 organisational change efforts that had culture change as an objective reported a high failure rate.[6] Culture change was most often undertaken because of competition and changes in customer demands. Success was more likely when the sponsors were perceived to be mid-level rather than senior executives; failure correlated most strongly with ineffective leadership and clashes with the existing culture. The study indicated that the success factors and barriers for cultural change resembled the profile of other types of organisational change. Again we see the important link between the external environment, internal capabilities and leadership setting the agenda for change.

By this time you may be thinking: Why bother? Can I make a difference? Does the world care? Do not despair. True, it is important to acknowledge that change that creates substantial value is hard; it means restructuring or even transforming the

[3] Ruef, M. (1997) 'Assessing Organizational Fitness on a Dynamic Landscape: An Empirical Test of the Relative Inertia Thesis', *Strategic Management Journal*. Ruef was at Stanford in 1997; today he's an associate professor at Princeton.

[4] Meyer, A., Goes, J.B. and Brooks, G.R. (1994) 'Organisations reacting to hyper turbulence', in Huber, G.P. and Glick, W.H. (eds), *Organizational Change and Redesign: Ideas and Insights for Improving Performance*, pp.66–111, Oxford University Press, New York.

[5] See Whittington, R., Pettigrew, A., Peck, S., Fenton, E. and Conyon, M. (1999) 'Change and Complementarities in the New Competitive Landscape: A European Panel Study, 1992–1996', *Organization Science*, 10, 5, pp.583–600; Tushman, M.L and O'Reily, C.A (1996) 'Ambidextrous Organisations: Managing Evolutionary and Revolutionary Change', *California Management Review*, 38, 4, pp.8–30; Gibson, C.B. and Burkinshaw, J. (2004) 'The Antecedents, Consequences, and Mediating Role of Organizational Ambidexterity', *Academy of Management Journal*, 47, 2, pp.209–226.

[6] Smith, M.E (2003) 'Changing an organisation's culture: correlates of success and failure', *Leadership and Organization Development Journal*, 24, 5, pp.249–61.

organisational culture. But there is hope. Metaphorically, it requires checking the weather forecast, preparing the sail, ensuring your crew are ready and having the right person on the tiller.

During his time at the helm, Jack Welch steered General Electric through a massive programme of change, including divestment, M&As, the introduction of Six Sigma and a host of other culture-change initiatives. Welch showed how a well-developed process can create enormous value. GE has a successful and well-planned methodology for acquisitions, for example, which makes the journey as smooth as possible. Naturally, this involves paying careful attention to due-diligence issues. But the company also spends as much time on the integration of new businesses – and has a dedicated integration manager who lives through the whole experience until the integration is totally complete.

During the decade of 1992–2002, GE made more than 400 acquisitions, which generally showed improvement in their performance (see Figure 2.2).

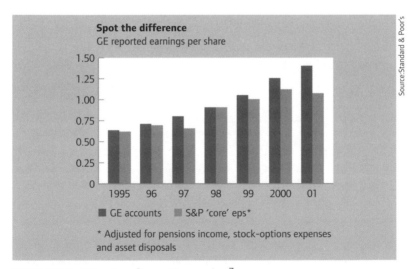

FIGURE 2.2 GE outperforms the market[7]

[7] *The Economist* (2002) 'Solving GE's big problem', 24 October.

GE is an unusual success story; it is the exception that proves the rule. What is its secret? A careful review of the GE approach shows that the company has developed change capabilities, which means it has the preconditions for successful change. In short, GE is set up for change. Indeed, under Welch, there was no alternative. When the arrival of the internet disrupted traditional businesses, Welch took readiness for change to new heights. He challenged his people with the mantra, 'Destroy your own business before someone else does.' The message was clear: change is the only way to survive. In this way, Welch was deliberately creating and provoking a culture that was primed for change. His successor, Jeff Immelt, has continued to foster changeability as a cornerstone of the company.

The in and outs of change

So why is strategic organisational change so difficult to achieve? Why do so many organisations derail? The simplistic answer is that it is down to the CEO. But while he or she is undoubtedly accountable, the CEO alone is not responsible. It is more complex than that.

Most organisations lack both awareness of the need to be ready and strategies to increase their 'readiness' capabilities. Understanding why things do not work is the first vital step to change a company's fortunes, and gaining that understanding involves considering what is happening in both the internal and external worlds.

There are plenty of books exploring why change fails. But thinkers on this enigmatic problem tend to reflect two broad camps – outsiders and insiders – neither of which fully grasps the issue.

The outsiders are those who argue that change is a function of external events and companies have limited choice. Their view is that industry-wide processes determine outcomes and survival, an outlook that leaves little room for managerial input.

The other side of this camp is represented by a host of methods and techniques in strategic management. Harvard Business School strategy guru Michael Porter, a representative of this school of thinking, would say that the art is finding the *white space* or strategic position in the market to gain competitive advantage. The emphasis of these approaches is *outside-in*.

The insiders form the other main genre on change. They see the answer as bound up with the organisation's internal dynamics. It may have to do with politics, conflict between functions, self-interest or hubris. Others within this camp position the problem with the dynamics or wisdom of the top team, the organisation's cultural barriers, or other internal processes. The central locus is *inside-out*.

My experience suggests that it isn't that straightforward! To really understand the dynamics of organisational change, you need to keep both perspectives in mind.

Ten reasons why change is hard

In looking at these two broad management perspectives, I have identified 10 reasons why change is a challenging endeavour. Five relate to the external world, five to the internal reality. The purpose of bringing these to your attention is not to depress you even further – quite the opposite. The purpose is to give you greater insights and help you avoid making the same mistakes that others have made. These are the external winds that you need to understand and internal resources that you need to get right before you even start the journey. Most companies have already hit the first big wave before they realise they left the port ill-prepared. To be forewarned is to be forearmed.

The internal factors

First, let's consider internal factors. The internal world of the organisation is a function of managerial and organisational competencies. The question is whether the organisation has the internal dynamic capabilities to change? Academics and consultants have identified five potential derailers:

1 **Blind spots** can cause leadership teams to miss the thing right in front of them.[8] One vivid example is the United States' decision to continue flying the Space Shuttle *Challenger*. With hindsight, there

[8] See Simon, H.A. (1955) 'A Behavioural Model of Rational Choice', *Quarterly Journal of Economics*, 69, pp.99–118; and Kahneman, D. and Tversky, A. (1979) 'Prospect Theory: An Analysis of Decision under Risk', *Econometrica*, 47, 2, pp.263–92

was overwhelming evidence to show that it was the wrong decision. For examples of the consequences in business, consider large-scale infrastructure projects that underestimate costs: London's Olympic Stadium for 2012, Boston's Big Dig transportation tunnel, the Channel Tunnel between the UK and France.

2 **Politics, self-interest, and emotions** – the people factor and the escalation of commitment mean that people within organisations find it difficult to change.[9] Legacies that have a history based on relationships, rituals and unspoken assumptions carry on regardless, long after the valid reasons that created them in the first place.

3 **Poor organisational routines** and a culture that is closed to learning new habits – or that even includes conflicting corporate cultures.[10] Experts in mergers and acquisitions often put the problems of gaining synergies down to the people factor and an inability to get the best out of competing cultures. There are countless examples of culture clashes in mergers, from PricewaterhouseCooper consultants being integrated with IBM to the differences between BMW and Rover Group, which was eventually sold a few years later for £10.

4 **Structural inertia**. Organisations are essentially stable social systems. That makes them efficient and reliable – but also leads to structural inertia. So, when change is necessary, nothing happens. For example, take a slow, post-merger integration. What happens in the first 100 days after the deal is closed is critical; it sets the tone for the integration process. Moving too slowly allows natural inertia to set in as well as loses the company money from the deal on a daily basis.[11]

---

[9] A classic on emotions and resistance is Coch,L. and French, R.P. (1948) 'Overcoming Resistance to Change', *Human Relations*, 1, pp.512–32; and on politics includes French, J.R.P. and Raven, B. (1959) 'The Basis of Social Power' in Cartwright, D. and Zander, A. (1960) *Group Dynamics: Research and Theory*, Tavistock Publications, London. See also Bain, A. (1998) 'Social Defences against Organisational Learning', *Human Relations*, 51, 3, pp.413–29 and Vince, R. (2001) 'Power and emotions in organisational learning', *Human Relations*, 54, 10:13, pp.1325–51.

[10] Levitt, B. and March, J. (1988) 'Organisational Learning', *Annual Review of Sociology*, 14, pp.319–40.

[11] Discussion on structural inertia suggests that it may be due to nature of the external dependencies, internal politics, over-commitment to existing opportunities or a lack of transparency in the structure and culture of the organisation.

5 **Poor implementation and project management**, if any at all.[12] Studies show that executives often are unsure what to do when faced with change. It is usually something that is delivered top-down, and they have no sense of competence or control over their destiny. They meander around wondering what to do next. Sound familiar? In one of the companies we worked with, an extensive, worldwide survey showed that 69 per cent of managers had neither the skills nor the confidence to implement change. Managers need tool kits, processes, frameworks and a set of core skills for change.

The external factors

Now, let us turn our attention to the external factors. These may be outside of your direct control, but you can influence them. Essentially, these external dependencies change the rules of the game and the way companies create value. Often, when external factors threaten, the challenge is: change or die. There are a number of different types of external challenge. They include the following five:

1 **Failure to keep up with changes in disruptive technology.**[13] For example, Polaroid's failure to respond to the threat of digital photography led directly to the company's demise. Failing to keep pace with changes in your industry can take you by surprise and lead to competitive advantage suddenly disappearing. Look at how IBM lost its advantage in its traditional hardware market. Even so, it is a positive role model for what can be achieved through change – witness its reinvention over the past decade from hardware to consulting.

2 **Reliance or dependency on other organisations for crucial resources or assets**. Think of outsourcing: you can find yourself locked into particular situations and expectations, in which who owns what and who is responsible for what may be impossible to establish. This happens more regularly than you might think. A rail company with which I worked had previous and legacy investments which meant that the infrastructure was slow to

[12] Brown, S. and Eisenhardt, K.M. (1997) 'The Art of Continuous Change: Linking Complexity Theory and Time-paced Evolution in Relentlessly Shifting Organizations', *Administrative Science Quarterly*, 42, pp.1–34.

[13] Romanelli, E. and Tushman, M.L. (1994) 'Organizational Transformation as Punctuated Equilibrium: an Empirical Test', *Academy of Management Journal*, 37, 5, pp.1141–66.

respond to new demands in transport.[14] The company couldn't do what it wanted.

3 **Political and legislative demands** can leave you out in the cold. Deregulation in the US airline industry led to established companies such as TWA failing to survive. The Sarbanes-Oxley Act of 2002 increased industry concentration among the major US accounting firms. Privatisation in some countries is a shock to the system for public sector organisations.

4 **Underestimating increasing competition from unexpected places**. Many petrol stations now offer food, for example, and compete directly with small grocery shops. Microsoft developed the Xbox in part to stop Sony coming into its space through the back door of the online Sony PlayStation. It did the same in bidding for Yahoo! against Google, which is considerably smaller but perceived as a strategic threat. Some of the biggest threats to financial-service organisations in the United Kingdom come from large supermarkets like Asda, Tesco and Marks & Spencer. These high-street brands can offer retail lending to consumers much more easily than traditional channels.

5 **Environmental volatility**, market and economic trends, and other contingencies affect your fortunes. These can range from the credit crunch where we saw a series of once regarded CEOs get fired – Chuck Prince of Citicorp, Stan O'Neal of Merrill Lynch and Jimmy Cayne of Bear Sterns – to business recovery or contingency planning due to war in neighbouring countries or the fear of a terrorist attack. Some people argue that the environment is everything. Individual firms have little or no control over their fortunes, and it is industry or economic shock waves that finally determine those parts of the market that survive and those that die. Ask Lehman Brothers.

Increasing your chances of success

What often connects the internal and external factors is another factor: a lack of strategic goals for change. Without the big strategic planks and the road map that follows, change is impossible to achieve. The strategic goal sets the compass for change and provides a beacon for the organisation to steer by.

[14] See Haverman, H.A. (1992) 'Between a Rock and a Hard Place: Organizational Change and Performance under Conditions of Fundamental Environmental Transformation', *Administrative Science Quarterly*, 37, pp.48–75 for more discussion.

The typical responses to these challenges are either strategic management or organisational development. One focuses on the external dynamics, the other on addressing the internal issues. These may take many forms. In the realm of strategy, for example, it might involve using Michael Porter's Five Forces of strategic analysis; or it might be following the five (or seven or ten steps) of the internal-change proponents such as John Kotter or Clayton Christensen. Each of these approaches can provide some of the solution. However, if, as I believe, change is about aligning external and internal issues, then by definition these approaches miss a critical dimension. An integrated approach that takes account of both the world in which the organisation operates and its internal capabilities provides a course to organisational change.

The model of change here builds on the existing research and tools, my own consulting practice and our research over the past five years.

> Internal Capability + External Conditions + Leadership = Changeability

The rest of this book explains the key concepts you need to understand and to assess your readiness for change. It turns stumbling blocks into pathways for success. It will enable you to identify your bench strength on the core internal capabilities and develop action steps to build these for further change. You will also get a view of your external world – how stable or volatile it is – and learn how to span the two.

The integration of your internal capability and the dynamics of your organisational context provide four clear strategies for change.

The first question, then, is: how ready *are* you for change?

> Take the test now in Appendix 2. The questionnaire diagnoses your organisation's readiness and with the help of the following chapters provides insights and ideas on what you need to do to improve your organisation's changeability. A full version of the questionnaire that allows you to benchmark your scores with other companies is available at: **www.ilyasjarrett.com**.

Summary

▌ Change is hard. Most large-scale, organisational change efforts fail. Less than 30 per cent succeed.

▌ The stumbling blocks that make change hard cluster around three main areas:

  1 The turbulence of the external environment, disruptive technology or unexpected changes in legislation can sweep away the company. The company may find itself no longer in balance with its context. Overwhelmed by discontinuity in its environment, it crashes into the rocks of despair along with other companies in that niche.

  2 Poor strategic leadership in the upper echelons of the organisation can be a serious problem. Blind spots can lead to insufficient environmental scanning for information and poor sense-making once they have the information. The result can lead to ruin.

  3 Inertia kills change. Organisations burdened with a culture that is averse to new ideas, that operate in silos and lack implementation skills are more likely to scupper change.

▌ Despite the various popular models of how to implement change, the results fundamentally do not improve. Study after study conveys the same clear message.

Successful change requires an integrated approach of looking out and looking in. Together these form a firm foundation for organisational change.

Are you ready to change?

It is better to travel well than to arrive.

Buddha

What is the best way to manage large and unpredictable risks? This was the issue that focused the minds and energies of specialists and managers at Swiss Re, one of the world's largest reinsurance companies. It was an interesting problem. How could unusual risks be underwritten by placing them back on the open financial markets? Hurricanes in Florida or floods in the Indian subcontinent are infrequent but major events. Techniques in alternative risk transfers marked a small but new territory, and the group had restructured to make its mark there. The company set up the Financial Services Business Group (FSBG) in 2001, and an integration programme swiftly followed to capture the benefits as quickly as possible.[1] Most commentators agreed there was scope for these types of products, but mobilising the market would not be easy. Every minute mattered.

FSBG set up a small change team to make the transition as smooth as possible. Jacques Aigrain, head of the group, did all the right things to start with: he set out the strategy with his top team, and created an organisational structure to draw on the advantages of the group's core competencies in reinsurance and investment banking.

[1] The material for this case was originally written for the London Business School consulting elective by the author with Jeff Mack and Cheryl Mayo of Swiss Re.

The agenda for change was clear, and working with the internal change team we started to go through the usual step models of change: creating a sense of urgency, building a guiding coalition and so on. But I quickly found that the models simply did not fit the reality of this complex change. It was not enough: step models get you only so far.

The mythology of steps

The myth of change is that it can be done in a series of steps. This assumes it is a planned process and that it can be controlled. Our experience at Swiss Re was quite the reverse. The process was interactive, complex, and nonlinear, undermining all of the traditional assumptions of change management. Emotions ran high, as did some of the political machinations. This experience is not unusual. In fact, it is typical of my experiences of most change initiatives. Change, I have found, is emergent. It is political; it cannot be controlled.[2] The dominant models in use fail to take account of these subtle aspects.

I realised that, for future projects, we needed to take a broader view of change. So shortly after coming off that assignment, I set out to re-examine my ideas. With some colleagues, I developed a change questionnaire to get more information and conducted it with a small number of companies to see what they thought were the key elements of change.

A short review of the books on change confirmed my suspicions. Historically, top-down, programmatic and planned change has been a successful model – after all, it worked for Stalin and Mao. This view of change is based on fundamental assumptions about the world: stability, certainty, homogeneity and centralised sources of power and authority. The trouble is that we now live in a fast-changing, post-modernist world in which complexity, uncertainty and difference are the norm. Sources of power as well as

---

[2] Taleb, N. N. (2007) *The Black Swan: The Impact of the Highly Improbable*, Allen Lane, London; and on the unpredictability and nonlinearity of change see Jarrett, M.G. (2005) 'The Seven Myths of Change', *Business Strategy Review*, 14, 4, pp.22–9.

expectations of employees and consumers have shifted; today, emergent, interactive processes yield results.

> Avoid using a simple steps-model approach. It cannot account for the complexities of change

The world has changed, and our models of change need to incorporate the systemic and interactive dynamics nature of the process. They should be adaptive. UK management professor Ralph Stacey argues that change is nonlinear and is a more complex process than we may think.[3] Similarly, in the context of culture change, top-down change created unexpected or unintended outcomes, again due to interactions throughout the system.[4] Others also share this point of view.[5]

What does this tell us? We are living in a world where the environmental landscape can shift quickly and unexpectedly. Models of change that use recipes provide useful frameworks but are insufficient. They can be static, unresponsive to outside influences and oversimplified. They can miss many of the subtleties and undercurrents of changes. In some cases, following these steps can do more harm than good. Thus, change models need to be contingent upon a firm understanding of the external environment and a grasp of your internal choices. Change is a function of external dynamics and internal capabilities – and, significantly, success or failure is often determined by the interaction between the two.

[3] Stacey, R. (1996) 'Management and the science of complexity: if organizational life is non-linear, can business strategies prevail?', Research and Technology Management, 39, 3, pp.2–5; and Stacey, R. (1993) Managing Chaos, Kogan Page, London.

[4] Harris, L.C. and Ogbonna, E. (2002) 'The unintended consequences of culture interventions: a study of unexpected outcomes', British Journal of Management, 13, pp.31–49.

[5] A broader critique of linear models of change and use of complexity theory can be found in Litchenstein, B.M (1996) 'Evolution or transformation: a critique and alternative to punctuated equilibrium', in Moore, D. (ed). Academy of Management Best Paper Proceedings, pp.291–5 (Academy of Management, Vancouver); Sammut-Bonnici, R. and Wensley, R. (2002) 'Darwinism, probability and complexity: market-based organizational transformation and change explained through the theories of evolution', International Journal of Management Reviews, 4, 3, pp.291–315.

British Airways – the ailing years

Let's look at an example. In the years after its privatisation in 1987, British Airways established a track record of successful change. The company's fortunes soared, making it, for a while, one of the world's most profitable airlines. By 1997, though, the nature of the challenge had shifted. Competition had increased, and not just from incumbent national airlines such as Lufthansa and Air France. BA also faced fierce competition from low-cost airlines such as Ryanair. Furthermore, fuel costs were increasing and the pound was high. This affected margins, travel patterns and morale. The task for newly installed CEO Bob Ayling was to reduce annual costs by £1 billion within three years.

But that wasn't all. BA's brand and reputation for corporate integrity had been tarnished by allegations of a dirty-tricks campaign against Virgin, and Ayling was taking heat for the decision to drop the Union Jack from the tail fins of the aircraft, replacing it with a series of global designs. Many in the British press saw the change as frivolous and even unpatriotic.

The need to change was indisputable, but Ayling faced a far more difficult situation than in the 1980s – one that was multidimensional, interdependent and complex. To make matters worse, labour relations continued to decline as he took on the unions. Ayling tried to restructure BA's pay system and overtime allowances for cabin staff. The idea was to reduce overheads and run a leaner and more cost-effective service. Most shareholders would have agreed that it was a good strategy for change. Unfortunately, a good plan was not enough. Two major disputes led to a three-day strike of 300 cabin crew members in July 1997, with another 2,000 taking sick leave through the summer. The effect was long-term disruption and an estimated loss of £125 million.

Copying change

No one said change was easy. Yet it is not the same for every manager, leader or company.

In 2001, when Anne Mulcahy took over as Xerox's first female CEO, the company was in dire straits, with annual losses of a third of a billion dollars, $17.1 billion in debts and rapidly falling debt ratings. Revenues were respectable, but a wave of new technology was about to hit hard on the bow. Competitors had stolen a march on digital products over the company's analogue legacy, and the threat of bankruptcy loomed. The year before, Xerox's stock price had crashed from a high of $64 to $4.43.

The previous CEO, Rick Thoman, formerly CFO at IBM, was fired after just 13 months in the job, unexpectedly handing Mulcahy the tiller. She had to become the leader of change and work through the mounting challenges. The change agenda was clear: streamline a bloated company – but not too much. Instructions to her change agent, Ursula Burns, were straightforward. Keep the company going. Don't ask anybody to do what you wouldn't do. Make sure we come out of this with a company our kids could benefit from. 'Go away and figure out how to get $2 billion out.'[6]

So what did they do? Mulcahy built a top team that operated as the organisation's head, heart and hands. CFO Larry Zimmerman worked the numbers, aided by the razor-sharp intellect of Jim Firestone, who ran North American operations. Ursula Burns was the hands, carefully implementing difficult cuts while trying to build the new company. The CEO held the heart of the organisation. Mulcahy's motto was to stay close to the values of the company:

> 'I'm what you call a "lifer" at Xerox; I've been with the company for 30 years,' she told *Business 2.0* in 2006. 'I stayed because I became enthralled by a culture that broadly defined "citizenship" to include how you treat your people, your customers, your suppliers, and the communities where we work and live. It wasn't talk. It was action, and still is. More than 40 years ago, our founder, Joe Wilson, spelled out a set of core values that cover how we engage with employees and customers, how we deliver value, and how we behave. Every decision I make is aligned with those values.'[7]

[6] Morris, B. (2007) 'Dynamic Duo', *Fortune*, 22 October 2007, pp.50–8.

[7] CNN, Business 2.0 How to Succeed in Business website: http://money.cnn.com/popups/2006/biz2/howtosucceed/7.html

Mulcahy held the top team together. Their closeness and ability to work well created the stability necessary to steady the ship in difficult waters. They met biweekly with no fixed agenda, agreeing to work on pressing issues and develop steps on how to resolve them.

Restructuring the company was a further key to survival. Xerox downsized from 91,000 to 58,000 employees. During the most difficult period, the CEO rallied the crew by visiting offices and boosting morale, creating a vision of the future and embodying the company's living values. As a longtime employee, Mulcahy had considerable credibility and plainly had the company's interest at heart.

Xerox developers created new colour products and management made a strategic decision to shift investment away from the black-and-white printer market. Mulcahy also moved to eliminate Xerox's lagging desktop-computing efforts.

Over a five-year period, Xerox was transformed from a moribund outfit to a fit company ready to meet its challenges (see Figure 3.1). It had halved its debts, increased net earnings to $1.2 billion, produced promising new products, quadrupled its share price, and experienced four straight quarters of operating profits. Anne Mulcahy's change programme was a success.

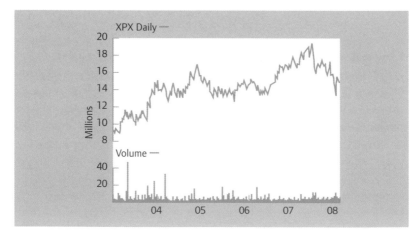

FIGURE 3.1 Xerox five-year share price: from lows of $4.34 in 2001 to $20 in mid-2007

Managing changeability

These two examples illustrate a company that was far from ready for change – British Airways – and one that had to become so – Xerox. What makes the difference? We asked real managers and leaders in business units around the world. My research team and I ran a survey of 5,000 executives from 250 companies across different regions, from Australia to Zimbabwe. It included financial-services organisations, pharmaceutical companies, manufacturers and a host of others. (See Appendix 1 for more details about the research.)

Using advanced statistical methods, we identified five critical internal capabilities that made the difference to organisations' change fortunes. We identified the difference between those that succeeded and those that did not: their *readiness to change.* By this, I mean the managerial and organisational preconditions and internal capability to change. We find these in the organisation's routines, processes and implicit learning.

The managers' responses suggest that Changeability can be seen in five managerial and organisational activities.

Scanning the horizon

Senior management teams that constantly scan their strategic environment tend to outperform their less eagle-eyed counterparts. They run constant radar sweeps of their surroundings, using a variety of data sources. Detecting new trends in the environment is often a stimulus for change, and it means that managers plan contingencies as the environment changes rather than waiting until the storm reaches their bows.

Making sense of the signs

Experienced sailors can tell a lot about the approaching weather by reading the clouds, changes in the wind and the subtleties of the waves. This is also true in the corporate world. Trends and data from the external environment need to be absorbed and used in decision making. Senior management teams that are able to draw accurate and incisive conclusions based on organisational routines and good judgement are more likely to achieve change. They are able to make sense of what is going on and interpret the implications of changes in their environment.

Creating a culture of openness

Organisations that operate at high levels of performance go beyond mere delivery. Such organisations engender open cultures that reward learning and creativity. Companies that successfully harness ideas create conditions that allow individuals and teams to gain synergies from working together as well as reap the benefits of focused chaos. They harness new ideas, diversity and ingenuity.

Weighing in the anchors of dysfunctional routine

Dysfunctional cultural barriers are commonplace in organisations resistant to change. People and culture are often invoked as 'derailers' of change.[8] These are the anchors that hold the organisation back and can often take the form of dysfunctional routines that are played out in the form of nasty politics, power struggles and the unsavoury side of organisational change – one in which people's self-interest, rather than the good of the company, drives behaviour.

Fluid execution

The results from the research found that the companies high on change also had high levels of structural coherence. Work processes flowed smoothly, communication around tasks was easy and silos were minimal. Conversely, companies that found it difficult to change talked of organisational silos, the difficulty of working across units and compared making change happen to steering a supertanker.

[8] See Beer, M. and Nohria N. (2000) 'Cracking the Code of Change', *Harvard Business Review*, May–June 133–41; and Ascari, A. Rockand M. and Dutta, S (1995) 'Re-engineering and organizational change: lessons from a comparative analysis of company experiences', *European Management Journal* 13, 1, pp.1–30, a study of 30 organisations' struggle with change; Smith, M.E. (2003) 'Changing an organization's culture: correlates of success and failure', *Leadership and Organization Development Journal*, 24, 5, pp.249–61, a study of 59 organisations' difficulty in succeeding in change.

Environmental impact

But that is only part of the story. The other side is the impact of the external environment. We know that the environment can determine the fortunes of change: it sets the landscape and dynamics of change; it forms the context for success; it can be a source of competitive advantage or threat.

Did you take the test to see if your organisation is ready for change? How do you think your organisation did on the essentials of change described above?

Changeability profiles

The research uncovered three statistically distinct organisational profiles. Each had different change capabilities.

First was a group with low change-factor scores (scores 1–3) on the norm scale. They found it difficult to change and were seen as *avoiders* of change. They were like oil tankers: slow, awkward and had difficulty in changing direction. Any changes were blocked, resisted or temporary.

In periods of relative stability, companies with an avoider profile can take advantage of the calm seas. Fine-tuning and incremental changes can help reap the benefits of structural efficiencies: but they struggle when the weather gets rough.

The majority of our sample fell in the middle, with scores between 4 and 7. We characterised these as *analysers*. They have a mixed profile and typically were unsure how to make change happen. They could tolerate moderate change. Cruiser yachts typify this profile: they operate well with current technology and can respond in a moderately strong wind. Typically, they prefer incremental change. The better ones, with higher scores, were more likely to deal well with restructuring change initiatives.

Finally, organisations that were good at change typically were strong across all of the five factors. Their scores were 8–10 on the scale. These were termed *adaptors*. Like racing yachts, they enjoy riding the crest of the wave. Pete Goss, the international sailor, aptly describes the rush of riding the waves: 'There is nothing more exciting than riding down a forty-foot wave.' Companies with this profile thrived on change, enabling them to strengthen their capability further through practice and adjustment.

Adapting to change

Adaptor organisations are perceptive of and receptive to change. They have internal systems, procedures and processes that almost run on automatic. The Mittal steel company has these characteristics. Lakshmi Mittal has grown his company from a fledging family business in India to the world's largest steel firm, Arcelor Mittal.

Starting from scratch in 1975, the company has always been vigilant in seeking out market opportunities and trends, and willing to expand into new markets and locations for its production. For instance, it foresaw rising Chinese demand for steel and seized the opportunity. Top management were clearly aware of market forces and developed a business model that was to prove highly successful: constantly evaluating how the company produced its steel. Mittal identified and used different technology, including direct-reduced pellets in its production steel rather than the more conventional model of imported billet or scrap steel. Another smart move: protecting the company's sources of supply by ownership arrangements around the world.

Mittal also acquired many failing steel companies that had lost money and which nobody wanted. It took over state-owned enterprises in Eastern Europe, smaller mills in the United States, and many high-profile and politically hot steel companies such as the European Arcelor.

Mittal's growth and success isn't just a story of unstoppable momentum and good fortune. He turned around its acquisitions by focusing on the process of change. What was the company's secret? It understood and redesigned its core capabilities. In Poland, for example, Mittal turned around its new company in one year. Clear metrics were set based on Mittal's high-performing mills. Management looked for process improvements and structural and inertial barriers – and broke through them. Mittal restructured and put in place new roles, responsibilities and processes.

The local companies had Mittal people who were assigned to the change programmes from start to finish to ensure that the new methodologies were understood, implemented and embedded. And this wasn't simply a parent company 'doing it' to the locals. The change processes involved and engaged local people – the managers who would run the plant once the turnaround was completed. In its acquisitions, Mittal has always instilled values and processes that make change work, building core capability and increasing the chances of longer-term performance and adaptability. This process is a key part of Mittal's winning formula and moves from just turnaround to sustainability.

Such companies constantly use the full range of change capabilities, and the role of co-ordination by the leadership group is a guiding principle of success. The marked difference is that insights and vision are carried through to innovative action and fluid execution. These companies gain the additional advantage of practice: the more they engage in change, the easier it becomes.

The danger is one of excess: using a sledgehammer to crack a nut, not knowing when to stop, or never taking time to build up and refresh capabilities when the wind lulls. Change may become a habit, something which occurs for its own sake, and the rationale behind it can become lost.

Change strategies for your profile

If readiness for change is the difference between organisations that achieve change and those that fail to do so, what can individuals and organisations do to increase the odds of success?

The simple answer is that the strategies for change depend upon your readiness profile and external conditions. Some organisations are better at change – the adaptors thrive on change. Such organisations have a higher chance of executing change initiatives.

Other organisations fall into categories that have an inbuilt disadvantage. The good news is that all organisations can improve their odds of success.

The rest of the book helps you decide what to do next. For example:

▌ It provides a deeper understanding of the dynamics of your scores and what may lie behind them.

▌ It introduces core concepts.

▌ It shows you what change means and the implications for your change capability.

▌ It provides examples of other companies, looking at what they have done, what you can learn from them and enabling you to understand that you are not alone.

▌ It shows what you need to do to make a difference.

Summary

▌ Strategic execution is one of the most difficult things to achieve. It requires as much thought and planning as the strategy itself.

▌ Thus, organisations that have the readiness and capability to change will have a strategic advantage over those that do not.

▌ Real change is deep and transformational. It is not enough to carry out a series of steps: change requires an approach that understands the integration of two perspectives – outside-in and inside-out. Few companies can control their external environment.

▌ Every company can decide to control, develop and build its internal capabilities. Our research identifies five critical factors that can make a difference to your fortunes of change. These managerial and organisational routines and behaviours make the difference.

part

Understanding your changeability index

Companies that learn from their experiences do better than those that do not. So to increase your organisation's changeability, you need to understand its strengths, challenges and opportunities. Each chapter in Part 2 provides a detailed description of the factors that matter and the implications of your SCi questionnaire results.

Please complete the questionnaire in Appendix 2. It diagnoses your organisation's readiness for change. It will also provide insights and, with the following chapters, ideas on what you need to do to improve your organisation's changeability. If you want to benchmark your scores against other organisations complete the full version of the questionnaire on the website: **www.ilyasjarrett.com**.

Why does the external environment matter?

The times they are a-changin.'

Bob Dylan

Prophetic words. Times have changed. But some things have not.

Shocked faces – anxious and worried – were the most memorable images. The queues of people seemed to go on for ever. Up and down the country, there were queues outside every branch. It could have been 1929, but it was not. It was 17 September 2007 and the bank was Northern Rock, based in Newcastle, in the north of England.

This was no small backwater entity. It had a million savers, 800,000 mortgage holders (including my family), 180,000 shareholders and 6,000 staff (see Figure 4.1). By the middle of 2007, Northern Rock held 19 per cent of the UK mortgage market, up from 11 per cent in 2006. It was the country's fifth-largest lender. And the bank's

Savers	1,000,000
Mortgage Holders	800,000
Shareholders	180,000
Staff	6,000

Source: Northern Rock, 25 July 2007

FIGURE 4.1 Northern Rock – the background

high-risk business model – dependent on funding from wholesale credit markets – kept it afloat as long as funding remained available.

Northern Rock had steady and progressive growth, with assets growing by a fifth annually. In January 2007, the bank announced record pre-tax profits for 2006 of £627 million, up 27 per cent from 2005. And then the credit crunch hit, fallout from the US subprime crisis. Looking to cover its likely exposure, Northern Rock was forced to request emergency funds from the Bank of England. The crisis led to the queues – and an overall loss of confidence in the banking system.[1]

After six months of rescue efforts, with Northern Rock's loan having grown to £26 billion, the government moved to nationalise the bank, absorbing costs of some £90 billion. The subprime crisis may have begun with low-income US homeowners, but it had a very real impact on a solid-seeming financial institution – and on UK taxpayers.

The Northern Rock story shows how a series of apparently unrelated events in one market can end up freezing the rear end of another. Our environment catches us in unexpected ways.

Leaders of organisations now operate in a rapidly changing environment. Gordon Brown, the British prime minister, would have turned pale green if he ever thought that a bank would be nationalised on his watch as PM. The irony was that he previously served as chancellor. A year later the contagion hits bigger fish like Lehman Brothers, Merrill Lynch and national economies. Such is the speed of change. The story shows how easy it is to be caught unawares.

All change

Dominant assumptions are no longer valid. New markets, channels and business models win over the tried and tested. Business as usual is not enough.

We do not have to look far to understand what this means in reality. Contrast a different situation. It is calm, you have a cool

[1] *The Economist* (2007) 'Northern Rock, Lessons of the Fall', 18 October (How a financial darling fell from grace, and why regulators didn't catch it).

drink in your hand, the sun is beating down on your back, and your bank comes to you. No, it is not exactly internet banking, and neither are you in the private lounge of a Swiss investment bank. You are, in fact, on the plains of Kenya, where bankers are using technology to make things easy.

One reason why it's hard to do business in remote locations is the lack of direct access to financial services. Branches are few and far between, and carrying large amounts of cash is obviously risky. Transaction and borrowing costs are high, hampering local entrepreneurs. The tide, though, may be turning. Technology has created a solution that leapfrogs existing barriers and the fixed costs associated with developing retail banking: mobile banking or m-banking. It tackles the difficulties of remote locations and building banking infrastructures – and threatens the model of traditional banks.

Safaricom, Kenya's biggest mobile operator, has made m-banking a reality. With the mobile telecoms company, Vodafone, Safaricom has set up a mobile-payment system called M-PESA, in which customers can deposit and withdraw money at Safaricom agents. Moreover, they can send funds to other people via text message, which recipients can 'cash' at agents.

The impact of such a simple system, using a device as ubiquitous as the mobile phone, can transform the lives of ordinary people. Casual workers can be paid by phone, taxi drivers do not need to carry cash, and payments by phone can be made to friends and relatives quickly by the press of a few numbers. No queuing, no bureaucracy. It provides speedy and safe transfers.

Wizzit, in South Africa, has gone one stage further towards being a virtual bank, offering 'your bank in your pocket'. With no branches, Wizzit allows secure payments and transfers via mobile phone and issues customers debit cards. It is aimed at, what the industry labels, 'unbanked' and 'underbanked' people. Wizzit operates in collaboration with a network of existing banks such as Standard Bank, First National and Nedbank, but you can get connected through a local individual agent – a Wizzkid – who will visit you and get you signed up. In providing a low-cost model for banking in the developing economies, the company could transform both the lives of a previously ignored group and the way we do banking in the future.[2]

[2] Standage, T. (2007) 'Cash on call,' The World in 2008, *The Economist*, p.135.

These different local scenes – mortgage markets in the United Kingdom and m-banking in Kenya – reflect a wider change in the world's connections and the impact of our economic environment. On one hand, the introduction of m-banking epitomises exciting and fresh developments that have arisen from changes in our business and economic environment. The combination and convergence of a number of different interests come into play. But we also see technology leapfrogging existing processes in Western economies that meet the needs of emerging economies. The change of winds provide both opportunities and threats depending upon where you are in the value chain.

Countries such as China are also investing more in Africa. For example, South Africa's Standard Bank, the continent's largest banking group by assets, is partnering with the Industrial and Commercial Bank of China (ICBC) in a transaction worth $5.5 billion. ICBC will take a 20 per cent stake in its Johannesburg-based counterpart.

African exports to China have grown by over 40 per cent a year since 2001, with imports from China quadrupling over the same period. Total trade reached $50 billion in 2006 and is expected to double by 2010. Africa is now the largest supplier of oil to China, and the region's markets represent an untapped market.[3]

Drivers of change

The vacillations of the external environment are the drivers for organisational change. The forces of change cannot always be seen, but their impact is felt through multiple drivers: climate change and the environmental agenda, globalisation, demographic shifts, technological change, and regulation/deregulation. Together, these dependencies make a powerful cocktail in which organisational change is a necessity for survival and sustainable growth.

If you don't change, one way or another, the following forces will change you:

[3] *The Economist* (2007) 'China and Africa, Running on the Same Range', 26 October.

The environment

Climate change is the biggest single question on the minds of our politicians, businesspeople, parents and children. What is the fate of our fragile earth? There is little doubt that the earth's temperature is rising abnormally. Average temperatures have increased by 0.74°C over the past hundred years. Around 0.4°C of this warming has occurred since the 1970s.[4]

Human activity adds to the problems of unpredictable weather, increasing temperatures and winds by the greenhouse effect. The main human influence on global climate is emissions of the key greenhouse gases: carbon dioxide, methane and nitrous oxide. The accumulation of these gases in the atmosphere strengthens the greenhouse effect.

Government reports suggest that mean global temperatures are likely to rise between 1.1 and 6.4°C (with a best estimate of 1.8 to 4°C) above 1990 levels by the end of this century, depending on our emissions. This will result in a rise in global sea levels of between 20 and 60 centimetres; continued melting of ice caps, glaciers and sea ice; changes in rainfall patterns; and more intense tropical cyclones.

There is no alternative: corporations will have to change. Standing still and keeping emissions at today's levels will not be enough. Emissions must be drastically reduced.

Some companies have already taken the lead, changing the way they design, manufacture, and market their brands and goods. Toyota's Prius hybrid is only the most visible example. The production and marketing of environmentally friendly and organic products has increased considerably over the past decade. For example, organic food sales have nearly quadrupled in the United States and in Britain are growing at about 30 per cent a year.[5]

---

[4] Defra website www.defra.gov.uk/.

[5] The Organic Trade Association estimated sales figure increases from $3.5 billion (1997) to $13.8 billion (2005) and penetrations from 0.81 per cent (1997) to 2.48 per cent (2005). See too estimates for Britain in 'Organic Albion', *The Economist*, 24 May 2007.

How are you responding to the environmental agenda? Does your strategy account for environmental impact? What would happen to your business model if energy costs were doubled by changes in legislation? As one manager put it: 'These are the trends we know about. But what will the world look like 10 years from now?' Who is really looking out that far?

Globalisation

It's a much-used word that I generally associate with protesters and marchers outside government buildings or World Trade Organization meetings – or with exploitation of children in sweatshops. Yet globalisation long predates industrialisation, much less sweatshops. Since *Homo sapiens* left the northern African plains the human race has lived with the threats and benefits of globalisation. The search for new resources, markets and opportunities is a natural part of human endeavour – just ask Marco Polo. But it is now about economics: the comparative advantage of each country's capabilities, with both pros and cons, depending on which side of the tracks you stand.

Globalisation means that the world is smaller and we are economically interdependent. It is cheaper to host your IT infrastructure in Mumbai than in New Jersey; it may make sense to source grapes from California rather than the south of France; investing in Chinese business may pay higher returns than its sluggish European competitors.

Economic trends suggest that a new order is emerging. Annual US growth rates of 1.5–2 per cent have long been the world economy's key driver. Those days are now probably in the past. A Goldman Sachs report[6] on the future growth and drivers of the world economy points to Brazil, Russia, India and China, which have experienced annual growth rates of 5–8 per cent. During the credit squeeze of 2007–08, they were the countries that propped up the world economy, as western economies floundered. Growth estimates for 2008–09 are shown in Figure 4.2.

---

[6] 'Dreaming with BRICs: the path to 2050', Goldman Sachs, Global Economics paper No.99, 2003.

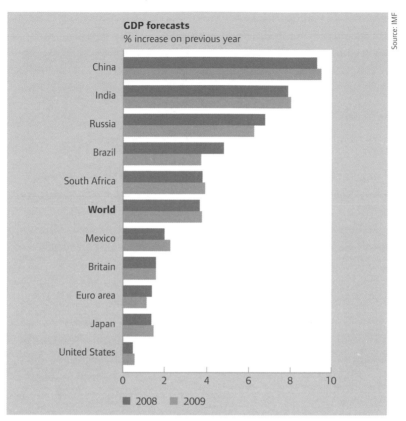

Source: IMF

FIGURE 4.2 Growth estimates 2008–09

There are also countries that grew 7 per cent, year on year for the past 25 years. Do you know which they are and is your company targeting their markets? They include Oman, Malaysia, Botswana, Brazil, Malta and Japan to name a few.[7] The tides are certainly changing.

This means new markets and different customer tastes, routes to market and channels. How will a luxury-goods company sell its expensive wares to Asian consumers? It also puts pressure on companies to be more agile; they will need to respond to these changes strategically and culturally in order to maintain any advantage. For example, Burberry, a fashion brand, has more outlets in Japan and Asia than in the United States and Europe. The company is responding to challenges of new and global markets.

[7] *The Economist* (2008) 'Economic growth, The winning formula', 21 May.

Sir Martin Sorrell, chief executive of WPP, started courting the Chinese authorities at the end of the 1990s. Many were sceptical then – and none of those sceptics are bragging about it today. Are you ready for this new world? Are you prepared?

Technology

Three trends are driving technology today: convergence, connectivity and convenience. In one small town in Germany, you no longer need to remember your four-digit number to make a transaction in the local supermarket. You only need one digit: your fingerprint. A quarter of a million people have signed up for this account, as have 3 million US customers for a similar programme, called Pay by Touch.

The mobile phone is also replacing all those small things you used to carry in the bottom of your handbag or pocket: your wallet, your book of contacts and in some cases your keys.

A technology called 'Near Field Communication' (NFC) has started to revolutionise our daily lives. NFC is based on shortwave wireless standards that we come across in contactless (no touch required) travel passes such as the Oyster card in London or the Octopus card in Hong Kong. The NFC chip is embedded in the cards. This technology chip can be inserted and replicated with mobile phones and used as a credit card wherever pay-stations are installed, which could be at cinemas, stores, petrol stations or any retail point.

In Japan, they are already leading the way. Some 20 million people use contactless Suica cards, issued by the East Japan Railway company. Card holders can pay for train fares, pay for goods in local shops and buy things from vending machines. Suica is one of many similar contactless and ticketing schemes in Japan. Some 40 million also use wallet-phones employing the NFC technology. Over 350,000 people have adopted mobile phones, which allow them to be used as Sucia cards. The balance on accounts can be seen on screen and transfers and top-ups to your account can be made via mobile internet connection. The same is also happening in parts of America, Asia and Europe.

The increasing penetration of mobile phones across the world provides a natural opportunity for technological convergence. Table 4.1 below shows that while penetration is high in countries like the United Kingdom and the United States, there is considerable opportunity to introduce leapfrog technology in the world's developing economies.

TABLE 4.1 Mobile phone subscriptions per 100 people[8]

Country	Per 100 people
Bangladesh	7
Kenya	14
Egypt	19
China	30
Philippines	42
Mexico	45
Turkey	60
South Africa	72
USA	83
UK	110

Some of these trends come together in various iconic products. Apple's iPhone pulls together fashion-conscious design, miniaturisation, mass storage and telephony all in one sleek, pocket-sized, power-packed phone.

These trends in globalisation and technology mean that sources of innovation can take place anywhere. More frequently they are in unexpected places and no longer among the US or European large companies. They take place in China or India. We know that software companies in India can be used for outsourcing and data processing. But this is to miss the real innovation of companies like Tata Consulting, Infosys and Wipro that have become world leaders in business-software services.

Innovation is also changing the pharmaceuticals industry. Tiny biotechnology firms are using network models to attack the markets of the dominant players. Asian competitors, like Ranbaxy and Dr Reddy's Laboratories, are no longer just followers of cheap generic

[8] Stantage, T. (2007) 'Cash on Call', The World in 2008, *The Economist*, p.134.

drugs. They are also concentrating and moving their focus to process innovation and drug discovery.[9]

These are huge leaps in the landscape. The leading companies of today are going to be those threatened tomorrow.

Demographics[10]

The pattern of our demographic changes appears uneven. Despite countries like China (1.3 billion) and India (1.1 billion) peaking in population, the world's population growth is actually slowing down. As more countries become rich more are seeing a growth slowdown. Even the BRIC countries (Brazil, Russia, India and China) are seeing a slowdown in population growth. Only sub-Saharan Africa has maintained fast growth rates.

From a market point of view the implications of this mean moving to new territories and marketplaces, and redesigning products and services to meet local demands. HSBC captures this sentiment in its slogan: 'The world's local bank.' Changes in customer tastes and local competition from these emerging markets will undoubtedly be a major driver for change.

Average child births are going down and people over 65 are living longer. So there is a change in the age profiles of workers and consumers. Better nutritional health, advances in medical technology and, to a lesser extent, better infant mortality rates help explain these shifting trends.

The demographics also see a shift towards non-OECD countries, with OECD nations experiencing shrinking populations and populations of working age. This has implications for labour, skills and talent but it also means a rise in the support ratio – those working who support those not in work.

[9] *The Economist* (2007) 'Innovation, Revving up', 11 October (How globalisation and information technology are spurring faster innovation).

[10] The inspiration for this chapter came from my colleague and economist, Professor Andrew Scott, who provided statistics and details based on his macro-economic lectures on demographics.

The macro-economic implications of these shifts are lower GDP because of smaller populations with a smaller proportion of working age. Governments will have less tax revenues and there may be less saving and, therefore, investment. So, in the longer term, interest rates are likely to be lower. Labour costs are likely to be higher and firms will seek to change their production and process methods to get better returns from their mix of capital – machines, building and plants – and people.

The ageing population is actually more of a problem for governments than national economies as it is projected that huge fiscal deficits will occur based on current policies.

We have had both generations X and Y. They both bucked the assumption of stable, job for life conservatism. Lifestyles, flexibility and personal challenge mark the basis of the new psychological contract. The trend is becoming mainstream. So a key corporate implication concerns HR practices and the need for radical changes to match work-life patterns

Regulation

Enron, Tyco and Worldcom remind us all why we have regulation in a corporate economy. It provides the economic checks and balances, maintains some form of fair play and factors in the social concerns of modern society.

But, the regulation picture is a mixed one – part Pollock, part Constable. We see both more regulation and more deregulation. It is hard for business executives to be clear on what is going on. A lot depends on legacy issues, sectors and the central government agenda. Institutional theories of organisation suggest that industry dynamics shape company's fortunes. Their dependencies upon new laws, and the social and cultural norms of their context, informs behaviour.

Take the Environment Agency in the United Kingdom. It regulates larger companies to ensure they meet legal standards and good practice of environmental care. However, smaller companies are exempt from the formality. Nonetheless, the outrage of a local community when one of these smaller companies polluted the countryside was so great that the offending company was forced to comply. Thus, regulation not only has a direct effect, but also sets the tone for others about expectations. We see the same increased expectation with the food industry and the role of the FDA on drugs. These moves are likely to increase and companies will have to change to comply.

The external environment matters. The environment is important because it is the context in which we do business and has a significant impact on how we do business. It can stir up unexpected surprises as well as opportunities. It upsets our dominant thinking and can also be a source of innovation.

These trends from west to east, large to small, mono-cultural paradigms to diverse perspectives will not cease. As the pace of change continues to challenge our assumptions about the world, we will be forced to revise business models, mindsets and behaviours. Fossil-free energy is not something we have yet really come to terms with. A world economy run out of the BRIC countries was unthinkable a decade ago. Imagine no air travel, only locally grown foods and population controls to match the earth's carrying capacity. These scenarios have yet to be debated.

There is no doubt that for organisations, a certain degree of uncertainty accompanies these shifting times. The credit crunch is a reminder. Those that manage, or better still anticipate, the changes will have an edge over their counterparts that could quickly share the fate of dinosaurs. Organisational capability for change is a core asset for firm survival, development and growth.

An OECD report states:

> 'Organizational change, understood as the implementation of new work practices such as teamwork, flatter management structures and job rotation, tends to be associated with higher productivity growth. Interestingly, productivity gains of firms that combine new technology with organisational change are considerable, whereas there does not appear to be much economic benefit in implementing new technology alone. In other words, work needs to be reorganized to use ICT (technology) effectively.'[11]

[11] Arnal, E., Ok, W. and Torres, R. (2001) 'Knowledge, Work Organisation and Economic Growth', *OECD Labour Market and Social Policy Occasional Papers*, No. 50, OECD Publishing.

The OECD research shows the difference between those companies that introduce new technology but no organisational change compared with those that do not. Figure 4.3 shows it is better to operate without technology. However, where there is a technology shift, then organisational change (NWP or New Working Practices), makes a significant difference with returns as high as 8 per cent.

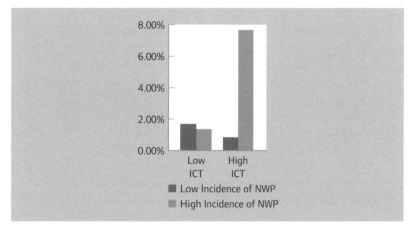

FIGURE 4.3 Producing growth US manufacturing 1992–98

Those organisations that are able to adapt steal a lead on the competition. Those that have organisational readiness start well prepared and slightly ahead of the game.

What are the major external drivers currently facing your organisation? List them and assess the impact they have on your need to change. These help answer the question: Why change?

Taking charge

High-volatility environments are fast-paced in movement. New features populate the landscape such as technology, new industry processes or unexpected competitors. Some companies will thrive in this environment. Others will crash as we saw during the new dot-com era and the recession of 2008–2009.

Stable environments have regular and consistent patterns associated with them. We do not see massive changes and any tend to be slow-moving. They engender efficiency and predictability. Stable environments can be due to national regulation, for example, that protects large areas of the public sector. It may also be a function of industry norms or practices. It took a long time for the legal profession to catch up with the mergers and global practices long established in other professional services firms.

Most companies or executives cannot change their environment. There are exceptions of course that operate monopolies or quasi-monopolies through the state, capitalism or a mixture of the two.

> Is your environment turbulent or stable? Look at the questionnaire in Appendix 3 and take the test.

The important point is that the environment gives as well as takes away. The art of taking charge is not only developing strategies that maintain your favourable positioning but also the strategies you take for managing selective and adaptive change. Both of these you can influence. Both of these make a difference. Both of these will increase the odds of success. Take heed of Dylan's prophetic words and avoid being a victim of these uncertain times and unprecedented changes.

Summary

- The world is a rapidly shifting but inter-dependent place. What happens in one part of the world will affect you in another part. We are a global village.
- The drivers for change are the environment's changes in climate, disruptive and technological innovations, demographics globalisation and regulation across the world.

▌ These lead to a constantly changing economic and business landscape that creates both challenges and opportunities for managers and their companies. Such dependencies affect the fortunes of organisational change as well as performance.

▌ These changes must be embraced. It is foolhardy to avoid them. It is predicted that such trends will continue and a strategy of avoidance becomes a self-fulfilling prophecy of failure.

▌ Managers cannot always influence their organisational environment. However, they can influence how they respond in term of the strategies for organisational change.

Does leadership make a difference?

The fault, dear Brutus, is not in our stars,
But in ourselves.

William Shakespeare

Where does leadership begin? Where change begins.

James MacGregor Burns

We cannot choose our external circumstances, but we can always choose
how we respond to them.

Epictetus

Ellen MacArthur is an extraordinary woman. In 2001, she
finished second in the quadrennial Vendée Globe race,
becoming both the first woman and the youngest person to
sail a yacht around the globe single-handed. Her record sailing trip
in the 60-foot *Kingfisher* was marked with vivid images of huge
waves, lonely days on the open seas and a very determined
woman. Winds of up to 70 mph formed the backdrop to her
journey, and at times she thought she would never make it. Tears
and fear, coupled with excitement and elation, created a unique
cocktail of despair and joy. Despite these extreme highs and lows,
the turbulence of the sea's natural rhythm, and the unpredictable
nature of the weather, after 94 days MacArthur beat the odds.
Having been named 'Yachtsman of the Year' at age 21, by the
British Telecom/Royal Yachting Association, she won an MBE for
her 2001 achievement – completed before her 25th birthday.

MacArthur knew the dangers and anticipated some of the difficulties. But she dug deep and had a clear goal: 'I started the race on 9 November with one objective – finishing.'[1]

There are similarities between the feats of sailing through the high winds and helming organisations during periods of change. The cold wind of the external environment is a major driver of company fortunes. New European Commission laws on carbon emissions can make a company uncompetitive as its costs increase. A shift in exchange rates can make exports expensive and reduce demand, while those leading the technology curve steal a march on their counterparts. This chapter is about helmsmanship and what it takes to steer through the storms of change.

The battle for the high street

The legendary British retail chain Marks & Spencer went through what could be politely described as a difficult patch at the end of the 1990s.[2] UK profits tumbled from an all-time high of £1 billion in 1997 to a disappointing £146 million four years later. Management was regarded as complacent, costs were high and the share price dropped two-thirds.

The rough waters of the market shocked the company out of its complacency. M&S was a great British institution: Margaret Thatcher and John Major – along with a third of the British public – claimed to have bought their underwear from the store. Stuart Rose took the helm in 2004.

Even the announcement of his new role was met with external turbulence, as he recounted in 2007:

'I met with non-executive director Kevin Lomax at 10:30 in the morning on Thursday, May 27, 2004. By 2:00 pm that same day, retail investor Philip Green, now Sir Philip, had signalled his intention to launch an £8 billion hostile takeover bid. By 6:00 pm,

[1] Interview with BBC, 11 February 2001, see BBC website, 'MacArthur re-writes sailing history' (http://news.bbc.co.uk/sport1/hi/in_depth/2001/vendee_globe/1158521.stm

[2] A variety of sources including *The Economist, Financial Times, Harvard Business Review.*

the company's bankers had asked if I could meet with the board the next morning.'[3]

Rose understood that he needed an approach that was outside-in and inside-out. Scanning the external environment, he quickly realised that the competition was fierce, fashions for the company's target markets were changing, and relying on the iconic M&S brand was not enough. Wal-Mart and Asda were fiercely attacking the traditional M&S market.

A review of the inside of the organisation helped Rose to realise that the company's drive for consistency had become a 'core rigidity' – a cultural blocker. The company had become 'old-fashioned'. M&S was slow, tied up in legacy and poor implementation. It was time to break through these organisational barriers. Rose had to increase the company's internal capabilities to change, taking out the fat and inefficiencies.

Rose had a turnaround on his hands, but he failed to fully understand the scope of the problem until he saw the books the weekend he agreed to become CEO. A self-described 'bricks-and-mortar man', he set out with a back-to-basics strategy agenda with three items: improve the product, improve the stores and improve the service.

He found ways to cut costs and increased sales by getting more customers through the door. On the cost side, the company re-engineered the supply chain so that it could compete with the likes of Next. Costs were slashed. Rose fired a legion of consultants that were all involved with 'strategic projects'. Products were rationalised and prices cut to increase competitiveness. At the time of his arrival, M&S had 16 sub-brands and over 35 weeks worth of stock, valued at some £3 billion. Set against only £4 billion takings in the first half of the year, the company had a serious problem. Its 'buy stock six months in advance' guideline was a legacy of the old days when M&S sold its own quality brand. Efficiencies and economies had worked well, but the fashion market was now moving so quickly that the company

[3] Rose, S (2007) 'Back in Fashion: How We're Reviving a British Icon', *Harvard Business Review*, May, pp.51–8.

bought too much and found itself with mountains of stock that it could not shift. Rose says: 'We had no choice but to sell it at a discount rate and take a hit on our margins.'[4]

M&S also off-loaded its financial-services business, which had been dogged with poor press and regulatory difficulties. Rose then focused attention on the company's core products. The entire management team helped launch the changes, from a new floor layout and refurbishment programme to a strong brand and advertising strategy aimed at the traditional M&S market: the middle-aged, middle-income woman. The team also bought in new products to increase the take-up of younger shoppers, including the womenswear brand Per Una.

Rose had to engage the management board, staff and shareholders in his recovery plan. Staving off a hostile bid from arch-rival Sir Philip Green, who put down an £8 billion bid for the company, Rose had to spend his first few months gaining commitment to his ideas and creating a sense of belief in his proposals. He managed to secure a stay of execution by promising improvements to the analysts and investors. The company gained £2 billion in value, and in January 2007 the share price topped the previous high.

Managing the complex network and dependencies of external and internal dynamics marked the success of M&S's turnaround. On the first day of 2008, Stuart Rose was knighted for 'services to the retail industry and to corporate social responsibility'. However, his journey is far from over. Slippage in growth of 2.2 per cent since 2007 over 12 months compared to rivals' growth of 3.2 per cent, a fall in profits wiping a third off share value and an attack on their market share means there is still more work to be done. Such are the fortunes of change.

Leadership teams matter

The Marks & Spencer story shows a management team's ability to turn around a company despite tough conditions. You can affect the odds of change by the way you respond. Without the support and

[4] Ibid. p.53.

alignment of his team, Rose would not have been successful. So how do teams like Stuart Rose's do it? There is far more to it than the familiar story of the hero's journey. He needs all the help he can get.

The environment is a significant determinant in organisational outcomes. However, researchers and academics suggest that it is the leadership group that can act as the final arbiter of environmental variability and performance. The leadership group's role is to manage the boundary between the external and internal dynamics of the organisational system. They form the guiding coalition that makes strategic and political decisions about the organisation's policies, direction and structure.[5] Managerial characteristics of tenure, age and their attitude and cognitive response to the organisation's performance will also impact strategic change.[6]

Management are the agents that Nobel economist Ronald Coase in 1937 dubbed 'entrepreneur-co-ordinators'. They provide routines for management practices and lie at the heart of decision making.[7] Their role as the 'strategic apex' provides thought leadership and competence to the rest of the organisation. They influence where the organisation is going, the culture and the conditions that help, as well as the other internal capabilities.

---

[5] Child, J. (1972) 'Organizational Structure, Environment and Performance: the role of strategic choice', *Sociology*, 6, pp.1–22; Cyert, R.M. and March, H.A. (1958) *A Behavioural Theory of the Firm*, Prentice Hall, New Jersey. There are a number of diagnostic models of change that explicitly link the leadership group with strategic outcomes: see Burke, W.W. and Litwin, G.H. (1992) 'A Causal Model of Organisation Performance and Change', *Journal of Management Studies*, 18, 3, pp.525–45; Nadler, D.A. and Tushman, M.L. (1979) 'A congruence model for diagnosing organisational behaviour', in Kolb, D., Rubin, I. and McIntyre, J. (eds) *Organisational Psychology: A Book of Readings* (Prentice Hall) Englewood Cliff, NJ.

[6] Boeker, W. (1997) 'Strategic Change: The influence of Managerial Characteristics and Organisational Growth', *Academy of Management Journal*, 40, 1, pp.152–70; Hambrick, D. C and Mason, P.A. (1984) 'Upper Echelons: The organisation as a reflection of its top management', *Academy of Management Review*, 9, pp.193–206; Cyert, R.M., and March, H.A. (1958) *A Behavioural Theory of the Firm*, Prentice Hall, New Jersey.

[7] Eisenhardt, K.M. (1989), 'Making fast strategic decisions in high-velocity environments', *Academy of Management Journal*, 32(2) pp.543–76; Eisendhardt, K.M. and Zbaracki, M. (1992) 'Strategic Decision Making', *Strategic Management Journal*, 13, pp. 17–37. The concept of the strategic apex of the top team can be found in Mintzberg, H. (1979) *The Structuring of Organisations*, Prentice Hall, New Jersey.

Studies show that the cognitive maps of our leaders – the ways in which they think – act as significant constraints, keeping them from seeing beyond what is in front of their noses. It is illustrated, for instance, by how long it took Polaroid to change direction: it took nearly two decades for the company once famous for innovation to shift from film to digital technology. Management believed and clung to the idea that R&D in the existing technology was important even though digital technology was gaining at pace. The leaders' cognitive and mental frames prevented adaptation until a new CEO stepped in and broke the dominant mental spell.[8]

The final piece of research which pricked my interest in this area comes from Stanford's Kathleen Eisenhardt and Mark Zbaracki. They undertook a meta-analysis of corporate decision making to determine the basis for their decision outcomes.[9] They discovered that most management teams are fundamentally irrational. Studies showed that teams made strategic decisions based on insufficient information, or that they were 'driven by politics'. The third but smaller category was 'garbage can' decision making: as the saying goes, garbage in leads to garbage out. Thus, how top managers perceive and interpret their context has a significant impact on an organisation's capability and mobilisation for change.

From our survey of 5,000 executives, two things stood out as making a real difference to those companies that were successful in change: how well they scanned the environment and how well they made sense of the data.

Scan your environment

Senior management teams that constantly scan their strategic environment tend to outperform their less vigilant counterparts.

[8] See Gavetti, G. and Levinthal, D. (2000) 'Looking Forward and Looking Backward: Cognitive and Experiential Search', *Administrative Science Quarterly*, 45, pp.113–37, a study looking at managerial blinkers; and Tripsas, M., and Gavetti, G. (2000) 'Capabilities, cognition, and inertia: Evidence from digital imaging', *Strategic Management Journal*, 21, 10/11, pp.1147–61 on Polaroid.

[9] Eisenhardt, K.M. and Zbaracki, M. (1992) 'Strategic Decision Making', *Strategic Management Journal*, 13, pp.17–37.

This involves using both external data – such as competitive analysis and customer insights – as well as internal and soft data, information they pick up in corporate corridors or through industry networks and grapevines.

The work of scanning should be done by the strategic apex of the organisation: those at the top and who span the boundary between the internal and external worlds.

The detection of new trends and subtleties in the environment is often a stimulus for change. It can help managers anticipate movements, preventing them from being taken off guard by sudden events. It also means that managers plan contingencies as the environment changes rather than waiting until it is too late. It is an early-warning system for potential dangers as well as opportunities.

Tesco, one of the world's largest retailers, is renowned for constantly keeping watch on its competitors' prices, strategies and moves. It is constantly aware of its changing environment and primed to respond. Each entry into international markets, such as Poland or the United States, is supported by thorough and extensive research of local markets, including researchers actually living with families to understand their markets. Helped by this knowledge, Tesco has made headway in international waters where other retailers, such as Marks & Spencer and Carrefour, have faltered.

Make sense of the signs

Scanning the environment is necessary but insufficient. Those at the top must also have the ability to understand, interpret and make sense of their organisational environment. Trends and data from the external environment need to be absorbed and used in decision making. Nobel economist Daniel Kahneman and Amos Tversky ran experiments to see how far people were willing to explore ideas outside of their personal mindsets. When presented with puzzles to stretch their critical thinking, most subjects tended to choose options that confirmed their 'natural' or untested bias rather than those that offered disconfirming information. It seems we naturally operate with blinkers on most of the time.

Senior management teams that draw accurate and incisive conclusions based on organisational routines and good judgement are more likely to achieve change. They are able to make sense of the situation, accurately interpret the implications of their environment and consider alternatives for action. They are able to break out of the constraints of blinkered mentality.

In our research, we found that the majority of leadership teams fail to recognise or remove these blinkers. They remain trapped by their collective mental models and psychological anchors; they encounter the problems of bounded rationality, where knee-jerk reactions lead to poor decision making. Bounded rationality, a concept coined by Nobel Prize winning economist Herbert Simon, describes the behaviours of managers acting from limited cognitive and perceptional frames. Thus, they do not search for information outside of their experience; what they see confirms their natural biases, and their untested and collective assumptions become reality. These mental traps reduce the effectiveness of those at the top and therefore the chances of successful change.

IBM's arrogant view that no one got fired for buying Big Blue led to its downturn in the 1990s as the PC world took over mainframes. It took years for the company to recover.

Companies that have systems and routines that help inform leadership teams to make sense of their external world tend to do better in both leading change and managing performance.[10]

In our research, the organisations that score higher on reading the signs are characterised by faith in senior managers' insights, judgement and decision-making ability. Organisational routines that engender both scanning and reading of the signs tend to be led by insightful top teams as opposed to ignorant ones, where their managerial systems can fail to do either.

Companies good at both scanning and reading the signs are better equipped for change. They are able to detect and then understand the implications of what is happening around them. These early-

---

[10] Boeker, W. (1997) 'Strategic Change: The Influence of Managerial Characteristics and Organisational Growth', *Academy of Management Journal* 40, 1, pp.152–70.

warning systems and routines allow them to mobilise their other internal resources and be prepared for change. These companies also allow space for regular challenges to assumptions so as to make better sense of the external world, leading to meaningful insights on organisational change.

Goldman Sachs, one of the world's most profitable investment banks, regularly challenges the dominant thinking and attitudes in the industry regarding risk. Most investing arms ask the question: Is this investment too risky? At Goldman, the question is: Are we taking enough risk? This strategy has provided the bank with a source of competitive advantage; during periods of uncertainty, it has paid off for them.

The reason isn't just luck. It is *calculated* risk. Goldman runs several outcome scenarios on its investments, crunches complex algorithms and draws upon the experience of its senior people in a panel that meets on a regular basis to assess the company's portfolio. Goldman's systems of scanning and sense making are both comprehensive and complex. If these boundaries are broken then as recent events have shown when a senior woman took too much risk, you are fired.

Other companies have similar programmes. Bill Gates and Steve Ballmer have steered Microsoft through choppy waters thanks to their insights, good sense and decision making. Microsoft's move into the hardware market, with the Xbox and Zune, was a strategic defensive move, as was moving to open-source collaboration. Both actions went against the company's initial strategic intentions. But making sense of whirls in the market meant these changes were fully embraced.

So what type of leadership do you have at the helm?

The leadership competencies of scanning and interpreting are shown in a matrix, see Figure 5.1. There are four cells: each with its own implications.

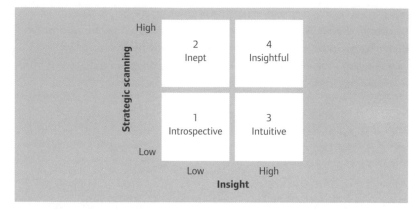

FIGURE 5.1 Top management groups can easily go astray – the 4i model

Cell one: low scanning and low insights

Groups in this cell might be (politely) described as 'ignorant'. This is a case of 'introspection' and 'bounded rationality' in which a lack of external input or quality thinking is demonstrated, leading to limited views of the external reality and potential options in the internal world. The group is inward-looking. Forty per cent of organisations fell into this category.

The Bay of Pigs debacle during the Kennedy administration serves as an example.

EXAMPLE

The Bay of Pigs

On 17 April 1961, a US-backed armed force of 1,511 Cuban exiles landed in the Bahía de Cochinos (Bay of Pigs) on the south coast of Cuba. Trained since May 1960 in Guatemala by members of the Central Intelligence Agency, and supplied with arms by the US government, the rebels intended to spark an insurrection in Cuba and overthrow the Communist regime of Fidel Castro. The invasion's planners, of course, failed to accurately assess the situation on the ground, and the Cuban army defeated the rebels within three days. During the crucial period of those early manoeuvres and exile attacks, President John F. Kennedy was called upon to launch air strikes but refused. He had obviously overestimated the strength of the rebel forces, and perhaps a fear of escalation stopped him taking things further. Nonetheless, this oversight meant that the rebellion would never achieve its goals, dooming the whole venture from the start.

Comparable corporate examples of hubris and poor planning range from Pan Am's sense of invulnerability to Enron's arrogance and misreading of its future fortunes.

Cell two: high scanning capability but low on insights

Here the organisation's strategic apex is in a state of 'denial' and ends up 'inept'. Despite the extensive information that is available, management's insights are based on 'erroneous assumptions', and thus the actions that follow are also risky. Fifteen per cent fell into this category.

EXAMPLE

IBM and the PC market

IBM's assumptions about its power in the PC market in the early 1990s illustrate the point. IBM was undoubtedly aware of the shift and rise in the PC market. Management were excellent at scanning; it was their sensemaking that was the problem. In many ways, their erroneous assumptions and blinkered insights led them to initially believe that PCs were going to tap into mainframes; they saw PCs as upgraded terminals rather than desktop computers in their own right. Thus, unwittingly, Big Blue accelerated the growth of the PC by setting the industry standard and allowing low-cost producers to clone them cheaper.

Cell three: low scanning and high insights

This implies that the leading group extrapolates from a smaller amount of data. This type of 'intuitive' insight or 'secondary thinking' can be correct. However, the risks and consequences can be high and unknown. Twelve per cent were represented in the sample. These 'intuitive types' may have more of an entrepreneurial flavour or be led by people who are well known in the field. Their leaders can lead by gut feel or instinct. The late Dame Anita Roddick is a striking example of a leader that led from gut instincts.

EXAMPLE

The Body Shop – creating a new paradigm

Roddick opened the first Body Shop on 26 March 1976, in Brighton, on the south coast of England. It was dramatically out of step with the cosmetics industry at the time and created a new paradigm for the industry – a resoundingly successful one.

In 2004, Dame Anita wrote on the Body Shop's website:

'28 years on The Body Shop is a multi-local business with over 1,980 stores serving over 77 million customers in 50 different markets in 25 different languages and across 12 time zones. And I haven't a clue how we got here!'

'The things that are now mainstream with the big corporates about the environment and human rights, Anita was doing those things in the '70s,' said Lynne Franks, the entrepreneur behind Sustainable Enterprise and Economic Dynamics. 'She was the first – she was the pioneer.'[11]

However, there is a cautionary note. There are several examples in which such an approach is not as successful. The futuristic but underpowered DeLorean coupe, featured in the blockbuster *Back to the Future* films, is an example of intuition gone wrong.

Cell four: high on both scanning behaviours and insights

This group would be described as being cognitively competent and providing on 'insightful' strategic leadership function.

---

[11] Rueben, A (2007) 'She wanted to tear up the rule book', Business Report, BBC News, 11 September.

> **EXAMPLE**
>
> ### Microsoft's response to change and threat
>
> Microsoft's leadership group read the market well during the 1990s and developed far-sighted web-based strategies. Over the years, management responded to changes and threats from Sony's PlayStation, Apple's iPod and Google's search tools with competitive products of their own. Their responses and reactions have been a result of good scanning and reasonable insights. Critics argue that if Microsoft was all that good, it would have anticipated these events. That's a fair point, and it further demonstrates that companies that do have a capability to change do not always stay on top. You have to earn the right to do so.

A surprising 35 per cent of companies fell into this category.

In summary

There are statistically significant differences between each of the categories, and thus, they do represent clear categories. Moreover, interviews suggest that these internal cognitive competencies are not the sole possession of the top management group and extend to those forming part of the network of leaders. However, the top management group will be the most influential group as they act on the key levers of the organisation such as strategy, structure and culture. They also are visible role models for the rest of the organisation.

Our results indicate that where top management groups demonstrate high levels of both scanning *and* interpreting behaviours, an organisation's ability to change tends to be higher.

Taking charge

How were your scores on strategic scanning and insights from reading the signs? If they were high, take comfort: you are already halfway there. Low scores are a grave source of concern, especially for organisations we might describe as low on both criteria.

What can managers do? Build scanning capability if your scores are really low, and constantly keep those capabilities exercised if they are higher.

Scan the environment regularly

▌ Actively use search routines; companies tend not to do this exercise that regularly. Once a year for the strategic plan is not enough.

▌ Ensure that the quality of the information is good.

▌ Use a variety of methods and multiple sources – both soft and hard data. Conferences are good for soft data and networks.

▌ Benchmark in areas of core capability, against companies other than your current competitors.

Typical tools for scanning include:

▌ PESTLE

▌ trend analysis of an industry

▌ SWOT

▌ market attractiveness vs. relative strengths

▌ benchmarking

▌ five forces

▌ value curve

▌ customer feedback

▌ scenario planning.

Make sense of the data

▌ Avoid groupthink, confirmatory biases and strategic blinkers.

▌ Challenge basic assumptions by incorporating new ideas and new people; bring middle managers to the strategic table.

▌ Employ reverse mentoring, as used at PricewaterhouseCoopers and Reuters.

▌ Use rigorous methods for decision making so as to weigh the probability of outcome and impact.

▌ Use outsiders to get another perspective.

Typical tools for making sense include:

▌ a prioritisation process

▌ issue analysis

▌ root-cause analysis

▌ critical analysis of events

▌ systems mapping

▌ decision-tree analysis.

Summary

▌ The ravages of the external environment can wreak havoc on your well-planned strategy: uncertainty, turbulence and instability rain down.

▌ However, the way that the strategic and managerial apex of the organisation responds can make a difference to the fortunes of change.

▌ Leadership groups that spend their time actively scanning the horizons of their landscape tend to be better at change, as they detect complex trends earlier.

▌ Leadership groups that are also able to make sense of and draw thoughtful conclusions concerning the information they gather are also more likely to drive change as they anticipate and mitigate consequences.

▌ Top management groups that do both are insightful. Such groups that display these behaviours and supporting routines are associated with higher-performing organisations.

6

How do you get people on board?

An organisation is a system, with a logic of its own, and all the weight of tradition and inertia. The deck is stacked in favour of the tried and proven way of doing things and against the taking of risks and striking out in new directions.

John D. Rockefeller III[1]

A group of five monkeys are kept in a cage under observation. Hours later, there is a loud noise and flashing lights, and a few bananas are thrown into the cage. The animals go wild with excitement, each taking what it can. The ritual is repeated. On the third occasion, they are hosed down with water as they attempt to go for the bananas. After a few repetitions of this process, they no longer go for the bananas. Other times they continue to be fed without the loud noise or flashing lights, and they display their natural enthusiasm. But when the signal comes, they hold back.

The experiment replaces two of the monkeys, and the same ritual starts again. The new monkeys see the food and leap forward, only to be barred by their fellow inmates. One breaks free and is duly dowsed. They all quickly learn the rules.

The routine goes on until all of the original monkeys have been replaced. So when the lights flash, the noise bellows, and bananas follow, not a single monkey moves. They stay in the corner of the cage. And none of them knows why.

[1] Quoted in Abraham Zaleznik (1992) 'Managers and Leaders: Are they Different?', *Harvard Business Review*, March–April, p.1.

This story illustrates how organisational dominant logic operates: implicitly and systemically.

Dominant logic

C.K. Prahalad describes it this way:

'The dominant logic of the company is, in essence, the DNA of the organisation. It reflects how managers are socialised. It manifests itself often, in an implicit theory of competition and value creation. It is embedded in standard operating procedures, shaping not only how the members of the organisation act but also how they think.'[2]

Dominant logic forms part of the organisation's bedrock culture: the immovable stone. Edgar Schein, the MIT professor and a specialist in the formation of organisational culture, highlights the unconscious nature of an organisation's cultures – the way it has provided a form of success in the past as well as the way the organisation sees the world and its image of itself. However, its recipe of success in the form of business models, processes and approaches to competition become embedded in the organisation and represent its underlying and basic assumptions.

A dominant logic can become a core rigidity that inhibits the organisation's people and processes to drive innovation and step outside the current paradigm. It can become 'faulty logic' and lead to organisational demise.

The challenge is to harness the cultural dynamics of success and avoid faulty logic taking over. Organisational culture and the 'people factor' can halt real change.[3] As a result, understanding what is going on is an important feature of change. Beneath the belly of the beast is a natural, dominant logic that operates in all organisations. The roots of these practices, implicit norms and rituals are old and well worn. They can be found in the vision and values of the founding and previous leaders and are left as legacies.

[2] Prahalad, C.K. (2004) 'The blinders of dominant logic', *Long Range Planning*, 37, 2, pp.171–80.

[3] Ascari, A., Rock, M. and Dutta, S. (1995) 'Re-engineering and organisational change: lessons from a comparative analysis of company experiences', *European Management Journal*, 13, 1, pp.1–30.

A colleague and I worked with the CFO and financial department of a public-sector organisation on a change initiative. The programme sought to change the basic assumptions and dominant logic from policing and bean counting to a performance and advisory culture. However, each time a new idea or process emerged from the group, someone would say, 'No. Smithy would not allow this,' and the idea was immediately dropped.

We were making slow progress with the organisation, running workshops, consulting to the executive directors and coaching individuals where necessary. A year went by, and we were seeing incremental change rather than the cultural changes the department and the rest of the organisation needed. We were baffled. They said they wanted change yet it was not happening at the required level.

A wet November morning and chance gave us an unexpected clue. We were met with scaffolding at the main entrance and were diverted to one of the side reception areas usually reserved for local council members. It had the air of being in the rare volumes section of a specialist library, and the hushed tones of the receptionist reinforced that this was a hallowed place. We waited patiently and started to examine the enormous oil paintings that adorned the walls. There, to our surprise, was a picture of John Smith.

In my excitement, I turned to the receptionist for confirmation that this was the said Smithy and commented how I had never seen him but felt I knew him well. She returned an icy response: 'Young man, you are referring to Mr Smith. I do not care for your tone, especially as he has been dead for 10 years.'

I was stopped in my tracks. Although bizarre, this story is absolutely true. The influence of Mr Smith was so strong that it clung to the organisation's being from the grave. It provided us with a clue about the respect that the company had for its elders and traditions. The story told us what was really important. It also gave some insights into management's faulty logic and how it prevented real changes from taking place. This informed insight opened up a new dialogue and helped to reframe the changes for today's world rather than the past.

Based on the 5,000 responses we received from executives, two factors help us understand an organisation's cultural logic: the degree of openness, a bias for new ideas and adaptation; and the extent to which the organisation engages in functional relationships and ritual – or whether these become destructive and dysfunctional routines.

How would you describe the culture of your organisation? List these descriptions and consider what are the features that either enhance or scupper change? Read on to find some of the answers to your questions on how to get people on board.

Founding leaders create strong cultures

Jon Hunt showed entrepreneurial talent at an early age. His first property foray came at the age of 19, when he borrowed a £100 deposit to buy a one-bedroom conversion in Woking, Surrey, for £4,500. Two years later, he sold it for £7,750. After a brief spell in the army, the young Hunt left for Canada, but came back to Britain where he found himself a job in an estate agency in Guildford, Surrey.

In 1981, 28-year-old Hunt set up a small estate agency in a converted Italian restaurant on the upmarket side of Notting Hill in west London. But the name for the company came from a small village close to where he grew up. Twenty-six years later, Foxtons had 19 offices in London, one in Guildford, new offices in New York and 1,300 employees.

Very quickly, the ex-army gunner developed a specific culture of the firm. Foxtons became famous for its fleet of colourful Minis, its café-style branches open 362 days a year, and its aggressive sales practices, which sometimes overstepped the mark.

The organisation is driven by a high-performance culture. Headline sales, strong pipelines and closing the deal are the big metrics. Foxtons deploy simple yet effective sales techniques to meet targets. Sales figures are typically updated and communicated twice a week.

Each office has a 'power hour' during which agents ring up clients and prospects to initiate, progress or close sales. Each week ends with a tally of individual sales figures. These are aggregated monthly, and sales reps get a ranking, which is publicly shared at the monthly regional sales meeting. Just in case you forget, the numbers are also posted to your home. High flyers are rewarded with weekend breaks, bottles of champagne, and – for the extraordinary performers – a classic red Ferrari on hire for a week. At the age of 26, you can own a BMW, earn double the UK average salary, and have a lot of fun with like-minded people. The only cost is your time: it is a culture of 11-hour days and weekends. The unspoken assumption is that the sky is the limit. It is a work hard, play hard environment, a combination of carrot and stick.

Many do not survive. If ten start on day one, six will probably leave within three months. The selection process is a form of social Darwinism. You attend an evening of about a hundred candidates, each being interviewed as if at some huge speed-dating convention. Of those selected, 25 per cent fall out within two weeks. It is a gruelling stretch. Poor performers can feel embarrassed if they do not make their numbers. The company looks for people who fit the culture, though, so it becomes a self-fulfilling circle.

It is not only staff that can get the rough end of this focused culture. The BBC programme *Watchdog* featured an investigation into the practices of estate agents and exposed Foxtons as complicit. Undercover reporters, watched by 4.5 million viewers, found that Foxtons' employees faked signatures on documents, a practice known as 'chop chop'. When Foxtons complained to the regulator, Ofcom, its petitions were rejected.[4]

Rupert Jones of the *Guardian* reported:

> 'For some, Foxtons is emblematic of all that is wrong with the industry. It became notorious for going in with high valuations to win business and charging well-above-average commission rates, and was fined four years ago for "flyboarding" – putting up boards outside houses where no sale had been instructed.'[5]

[4] Dowell, B. (2007) 'Foxtons' *Watchdog* gripe rejected', *Media Guardian*, 16 July 2007.

[5] Jones, R. (2007) 'He has built a business…', *Media Guardian*, 25 May 2007.

Yet, Jones conceded: 'Its success, however, is indisputable.' Others agree. Hunt 'has built a business on a model that I wouldn't want to replicate, but he has done phenomenally well out of the industry, and for that, you have to take your hat off and say well done', said Harry Hill, chairman of Britain's biggest firm of estate agents, Countrywide.

Foxtons was eventually sold to a private equity group for an estimated £390 million in 2007.

Talking to a typical manager in Foxtons they would say great things. The company is like a family. You form strong bonds and there is a sense of camaraderie. People help each other and there is a lot of support when you start out and are still wet behind the ears. Yes, it pays well, and the incentives mean you can achieve a lot of things along the way. But the thing that really makes a difference is that as a young person you gain a solid grounding in business education and become a savvy commercial operator.

Foxtons' dominant logic and basic assumptions are very clear. It is definitely a source of its success. However, the pitfall is that those same qualities can quickly turn into dragging anchors that stop change.

> Harnessing the talents and ingenuity of your organisation means understanding the dominant logic and steering it.

Two factors make a difference

Our research found that two factors make a difference to your culture: how companies harness innovation and collaboration, and how they counteract dysfunctional and debilitating routines.

Harnessing ingenuity

The best companies go beyond mere delivery. We found that they harness ingenuity through collaboration and innovation. These organisations create open cultures that reward learning and creativity. Companies that successfully harness ideas create conditions that allow individuals and teams to gain synergies from working together as well as reaping the benefits of focused chaos.

This is characterised by an openness to difference and diversity and a willingness to innovate and use conflict as a source of new ideas, deploying processes that turn ideas into action.

Sailing provides us with many lessons that are equally applicable to organisational change. I remember my oldest son, Jamal, learning to sail in a single-handed laser. I watched as he capsized time after time. It was in one of the Salcombe bays – and although summer, the water was extremely cold once you fell in. He'd emerge shivering from each lesson. But he never gave up. This paid off. By the third day he was a competent sailor. His willingness to experiment, learn from mistakes and enter the spirit of taking risks made all the difference. When the tide swelled up he was ready and tacking like a pro. Tenacity and openness marked his approach and he gained the rewards of personal satisfaction and winning the race on the last day of the course.

The same is true for organisations. IDEO, the design company in Palo Alto, California, is an exemplary organisation that does this well – so much so that corporations have asked them to help re-engineer their cultures.

Our research shows that some organisations engender innovative cultures, in which individuals and teams are more likely to come up with new ideas. They differ from those that stifle creativity in a number of ways. One important cultural aspect of innovative organisations is that they have a *high tolerance of failure*. This may seem counterintuitive. But innovation is unpredictable, and research suggests that people and companies that make more attempts to be creative end up with more innovations. It is not surprising that many attempts fail; therefore, organisations must be willing to accept failures. This facilitates a culture of experimentation and play – and encourages people to feel psychologically safe to take risks.

In addition to a tolerance of failure, innovative organisations are *action-oriented* – in other words, they do more than organisations that are not innovative. One way to encourage this kind of action orientation is to use prototypes to drive the innovation process. Prototypes tend to be most effective at promoting innovation when the prototyping is rapid, iterative and rough. Teams can waste time developing perfect working solutions, but rough prototypes help the group to communicate and understand their ideas and to identify flaws in them.

Finally, organisations with innovative cultures have *sufficient resources*. Time pressure and lack of other resources, such as financial support, tend to limit innovation. An innovative organisation will therefore build in slack in terms of budgets, planning and time, to give people space to play with ideas and develop innovations.[6]

Google is currently one of those organisations that demonstrate high levels of innovation. It has a 70–20–10 working model, where engineers can spend 20 per cent of their time brainstorming and 10 per cent on anything that is of interest to them. The popular Gmail application was a product of internal ingenuity. The model aims to stimulate creativity and teamwork by merging the line between work and play. Not surprisingly, encouraging a creative culture means that the company attracts bright people, and the virtuous loop of innovation continues. Marissa Mayer, vice-president of Search Product and User Experience, is one of the company's driving forces and champions of innovation. She instituted a challenging process that has harnessed and refined the best ideas and quickly tossed overboard those without long-term viability. Thus, creativity is focused.

Mayer says:

> 'Creativity is often misunderstood. People often think of it in terms of artistic work – unbridled, unguided effort that leads to beautiful effect. If you look deeper, however, you'll find that some of the most inspiring art forms . . . are fraught with constraints.'[7]

Talking to Arun Singh, a strategic partner manager at Google, she says: 'It's a culture that really wants to do things differently and think out of the box. It has a high percentage of new grads. It's

[6] Harris, S. and Jarrett, M. (2007) Working paper on group effectiveness and creativity, London Business School.

[7] Mayer, M. (2006) 'Turning Limitations into Innovation', 1 February, Business Week Online.

really like an extension of college where bright people work very hard to stand out.' The company creates a campus environment. Healthy breakfast, lunch and dinner, and even get your dry cleaning done too. All for free!

Procter & Gamble also provides a world-class example of harnessing collaboration and innovation. The company that's famous for products from Pampers® to toothpaste constantly scouts the world for new ideas, driven by a need for renewal. As a mature company, it no longer saw the steady rise of growth. Doing the same thing the P&G way, through investments in R&D across thousands of researchers, was not going to do it. Intense competition and the spread of new technologies meant trouble. The company needed to refresh and renew to turn the monolith around. Only 35 per cent of P&G's new products met the company's financial objectives. R&D productivity was stagnant.

CEO A.G. Lafley understood the urgency and size of the problem. Thinking it would take P&G a few years to get back into shape, he focused on the company's four core business areas (accounting for 54 per cent of sales and 60 per cent of profits); its big, established leading brands; and P&G's top 10 countries (with 80 per cent of sales and 95 per cent of profits). In addition, some 10,000 jobs were slashed and underperforming or non-core businesses were shuttered. Brands such as Comet, Crisco and Jif were sold off.

These were the conditions that turned things upside down at P&G. It drastically cut its R&D budget, letting go armies of internal researchers and analysts. The company developed an 'outside-in' approach to product and process development, which it has tagged 'Connect + Develop'. Lafley announced that 50 per cent of P&G's innovation should come from outside the company walls.

It was easy to see value in the economics. For every one of the company's researchers, P&G calculated there were 200 people – scientists and engineers – outside the company who had talents P&G could utilise. Instead of 9,000 people in corporate R&D, the company estimated that 1.5 million people worldwide had knowledge worth tapping into. Research and development was reinvented with an organisation of 1,507,500 people.

The whole concept works through active external collaboration through the company's Connect + Develop website (see Figure 6.1) and scouts who identify and network with technology entrepreneurs throughout the world.

Source:www.pgconnectdevelop.com

Could your innovation
be the next
GAME-CHANGING DEAL?

FIGURE 6.1 P&G collaborates on ideas

Weighing in the anchors of dysfunctional routine

Left to their own devices, most organisations find a point of equilibrium and settle. Inertia is the default. It is a function of the cultural logic and basic assumptions. The system's underlying culture, structure and relationships find the status quo comfortable – after all, it serves the interests of both the organisation and the people within it.

Let's assume that most people come to work to do a good job. Let's also be realistic and say that a small minority actively undermine change. It still does not explain the tendency towards inertia. There are two scenarios: one in which people unwittingly contribute to change inertia, the other in which people actively undermine the process. Contrary to popular belief, it is the first group that's the difficulty – we underestimate the size and scope and how embedded the problem really is. Let's consider why people 'resist' change.

The 'rational' response

It is said that people act as rational economic decision makers. They simply add up the benefits and cost of change using their own subjective valuation of the payoffs, impact and risks. For each potential benefit of a change, the idea of diminishing marginal returns sets in – each marginal benefit delivers less and less return.

Imagine you are really hungry after a long walk. You head straight for the fridge, pull out your favourite food, and stuff yourself. The first helping tastes fantastic. The second is good. The third is fine. After the fifth, you begin to wonder what the fuss was about, and very soon satiation turns to rejection, with each further helping creating discomfort and a negative response. This is the idea of diminishing marginal returns. Each helping brings less and less marginal satisfaction.

Thus, it quickly means that people tend to prefer the safety and comfort of the benefits they currently enjoy versus the marginal and perceived poor benefits of a change. So we can understand that they are not being awkward – they are simply making a 'rational' decision. However, this accounts for only some of the answer.

Behavioural economist Daniel Kahneman and psychologist Amos Tversky demonstrated that under conditions of uncertainty people do not act rationally. Change creates anxiety and plays tricks on the mind. People stop thinking rationally and instead use personal reference points, particularly the status quo, to make decisions. Kahneman and Tversky found that in a situation in which people have to give up current benefits they become risk averse. However, when the same odds are expressed in terms of *loss*, they are more likely to accept risk because they see they do not have anything to lose. Our risk preferences increase.

Kahneman and Tversky also show that personal biases, mental models and stereotypes consistently influence decision makers over rational statistical computation. People behave irrationally. They continue to invest time, effort and money into poor decisions even when new and better opportunities arise. They can become sentimental over possessions or ideas and tenaciously hang onto these despite the overwhelming facts. Human judgements take shortcuts based on personal biases. People's choices do not follow the rules of rationality.

Simply how things are framed can make a difference Stressing the potential losses during periods of change is more likely to galvanise action. The leader's challenge is to reframe the odds, which means asking, listening and thinking about the change. It means emphasising the benefits of change and the costs of doing nothing, depending upon the situation.

Emotions at work

Appealing to rational thinking is easier than the emotional side of change. Emotions scupper successful change. People do not enjoy change for a variety of reasons. Fear, a loss of identity and the loss of familiar structures and habitat are the most obvious. However, the shadows of emotions are rooted in a combination of our personality, experiences of growing up and previous experiences of change. One oil-company executive with whom we worked proudly stated that his children will travel from one expat location to another because that's what his father did for him and now he really enjoys change. Two things I would highlight. First, patterns from our parents shape our own lifestyle patterns, even if we do not realise it. Second, what was good for this executive may not work out so well for his children, who may grow up to fear change. The main point is that change is complex and pop psychology is not the answer.

Addressing emotions during organisational change is a key to success. This is one of the major stumbling blocks that most find hard to overcome.

Elisabeth Kübler-Ross's book *On Death and Dying* describes how we go through predictable stages of grief, often referred to as the transition or bereavement curve. One concept that helps explain the reasons why we find change hard and go through a type of grieving is attachment theory.

John Bowlby developed his theory of attachment during the 1950s.[8] Influenced by scientific methods, Charles Darwin's evolutionary ideas, and empirical studies, Bowlby set out to bridge the link between psychology and evolutionary ideas. He studied children's attachment behaviours through experimental studies, and since then much of the work in this field has followed this empirical approach.

The theory suggests that we form early childhood attachments to our parental figures. Modern-day thinking would not find this surprising: parents who are attentive, attuned to their children's needs, and able to provide emotional support tend to have children that are secure in themselves and in their relationships with others. In such cases, the children then are able to work through separation, loss and grief. They are able to manage difficult transitions. They are open to exploration, creativity and play. They are curious about the world. Where these preconditions are absent, children establish insecure patterns about themselves and in their relationships with others. They tend to be anxious, fearful of commitment in relationships, and ambivalent or confused about whom they can trust.

The shocking revelation about the countless studies that have subsequently been conducted is that these styles of attachment – secure or insecure – continue from childhood to adulthood.

Researchers conducted an experiment with one-year-old children in which their parents leave them on two occasions for three minutes each. The research assistant stays in the room on the first occasion and leaves on the second occasion. Researchers observed three distinct styles.

▍ *Secure* styles protest when the parent leaves, crying and screaming. On the parent's return, he or she is able to welcome them, be pleased, and start to play again untroubled.

▍ Those classified as *insecure* fall into two styles. The *avoidant* style defends themselves against forming attachments that they experience as unreliable. They want to protect themselves from

[8] Holmes, J. (1993) *John Bowlby & Attachment Theory*, Routledge, London, provides a biographical as well as a clinical account of Bowlby's work.

the pain so keep their feelings bottled up after the parent leaves and show little outward appearance of protest. Once the parent returns, they are cautious, vigilant and anxious, and do not re-engage well. Those with an *ambivalent* style tend to have mood swings. On the one hand, they really miss their parent; on the other, they are angry that they were left alone. So they can be both clingy and rejecting at the same time.[9]

In another study, children were then retested again at the age of 10 to find whether the patterns were still dominant: these styles continue.[10] When similar studies have been done with adults, the patterns persist. Peers tended to classify their securely rated colleagues as more ego-resilient, less anxious and hostile, and having greater social support than their 'insecure' counterparts.[11] Finally, the nature of attachment styles will tend to be highly correlated with the attachment style of parents. Thus, it is intergenerational.

A key idea in Bowlby's work is that the nature of the environment can provide a secure or insecure base. Thus, during periods of change and loss, these changes in our environment evoke dominant default styles that are based on our internal working models of the world. These are our assumptions and formations of the external world, which may be seen as threatening – 'nobody loves me' – or more reassuring. Our response is also moderated by personality and our coping styles, grounded in earlier situations that can become reinforced and embedded. The environment in which we operate can stimulate, modify or even change our default model depending upon the quality and security (or insecurity) of the setting.

In each of these cases, the notion of a secure base provides the opportunity for us to move on. It provides safety, security, an opportunity to explore and a space to gain confidence. Thus,

---

[9] Ainsworth, M., Blehar, M., Water, E. and Wall, S. (1978) *Patterns of Attachment: Assessed in the Strange Situation and at Home*, Erlbaum, Hillsdale, NJ.

[10] Bretherton, I. (1985) 'Attachment Theory: retrospect and prospect', in Bretherton, I. and Waters, E. (eds), *Growing points of attachment theory and research*, Monographs of the Society for Research in Child Development, 50, pp.3–35.

[11] Kobak, R.R. and Sceery, A. (1988) 'Attachment in late adolescence: working models, affect regulation, and representation of self and others', *Child Development*, 59, pp.135–46.

during periods of change, when such structures that the organisation provides suddenly disappear, it is not surprising that emotions run high and systemic change can falter.

Typical styles – some cases

Organisations, their structures, cultures, rituals and routines provide the environment for our work. We spend more time in the day there than anywhere else. We form deep bonds and relationships, helping define our role and identity. During periods of change we fall into typical secure or insecure styles.

> **CASE STUDY**
>
> ### Redundancy
>
> Consider Harry who was a senior partner in a professional service firm. The consulting market took a dip, and he found himself 'on the job pile'. He was distraught, angry and confused. He had worked for the firm for several years; it was part of his DNA. Now Harry was unsure what to do with his life. The company that had provided so much had now 'rejected and betrayed him' – such were his feelings of loss. His typical style of dealing with feelings of attachment was already insecure and typically anxious, often worried and expecting the worse. So redundancy was met with, 'I knew this would happen,' and, 'You cannot trust anyone. You have to rely on yourself.' He took the whole thing very badly.

In another case I encountered, a well-known family firm saw these themes played out in the problem of succession.

> **CASE STUDY**
>
> ### Succession
>
> The father was a successful but rather detached leader during the stable years of the company. His authoritarian and remote style worked for the whole company, providing stability and a sense of order.

His son took over during a period of rapid change. The market suddenly had more players, shattering the company's near-monopoly. Branding became important rather than production qualities, and internal practices were seen as delaying the changes rather than supporting them. The sense of change was so great for the newly appointed company head that he froze. The context led him to default behaviours that mirrored his father's remote style. The son clung to a past that he rationally knew would lead to the company's long-term failure.

The differences between the past and the needs of the present were then played out as rivalries between manufacturing on one side and sales and marketing on the other. These conflicts were so great that each faction actively sabotaged the other's initiatives, even though they knew the changes were critical to the company's survival. It took a new managing director with a fresh perspective to help resolve the matter. The task for those looking for change is to break through the treacle of inertia.

These cases illustrate how the loss of a secure base can knock us off track. In the first case, it impacted on the identity of Harry and caused real confusion over what to do with his life. The second case illustrates how leadership, culture and environmental demands can lead to a complex cocktail of attachment needs and acting from a script that you didn't even know was written.

You would probably get really upset if you left your favourite mug out and came back to find it used, dirty and covered with a ring of bacteria at the top. What would be your reaction? Well consider the loss of job, status, security and identity. The cost of a mug is a few euros. What is the cost of the loss of a secure base?

Individual psychology affects group psychology. Organisations comprise groups and individuals. These complex interactions form organisational cultures and a web of unspoken and unconscious relationships that play out in the drama of corporate life. Stop and observe. It will provide an entirely different perspective.

The minority report

Finally, yes, there is a minority within every organisation seeking to sabotage change. In our research, stories of cliques, the inner circle and shooting the messenger were often relayed as examples of what occurs in organisations.

Saboteurs must be confronted and rooted out as quickly as possible. They can act as a negative influence on the rest of the group and grow like a cancer on the marrow of the organisation. Cut them out before they spread and infect the rest of the system.

When Peter Simmonds took over managing a new section of a bank, he inherited a mixed team of performers. In particular, one of the longest-serving members of the group was not just underperforming but actively going against the grain of the changes. Initiatives for which he was responsible were never completed. He was always criticising Peter behind his back, and he encouraged and often led distracting discussions in team meetings.

Peter did not know what to do. He did not feel he had the same level of knowledge and experience. At 45, he was still junior in age. He had worked in the bank since leaving school but still had fewer years than his difficult colleague. Peter tried an informal chat but got nowhere, and the behaviour continued. He tried coaching; he tried performance management. There were some minor improvements but then things reverted to the previous state after a couple of weeks. Finally, after 18 months and considerable frustration, Peter restructured the business and let his colleague go.

It was only then that he realised what a destructive force this man had been. Stories came out about the full extent of his behaviour. Team colleagues reported with relief that he had gone and wondered why Peter had not acted sooner. These are among the most difficult decisions to make, but delay costs time, energy and focus.

Moving people with you

The art of moving people with you is understanding them, listening to them and finding common ground; in short, building strong relationships. Creating this network of bonds and strong relationships is known as building social capital. Studies suggest that those with high levels of social capital are able to do business easier, confer favours and have high degrees of influence. The typical skills include understanding and managing networks along with interpersonal and politically astute behaviours.

The people factor is the hardest part of change. How would you rate yourself personally? How were your organisation's scores on openness and positive, functional dynamics when you attempted the questionnaire in Appendix 2?

Poor scores lead to inertia and the lasting forces of the dominant logic can even prevail when the company is threatened by survival. Action and a sense of urgency around a clearly articulated vision are what's needed.

What can executives do?

▌ Set a clear vision and direction of the destination and why the organisation must change.

▌ Devise and implement an engagement strategy. This means that you have to ask and listen to what really matters to your people as they make the change transition, and plan how they will be involved.

▌ Emphasise the benefits of the change in terms specific to the people involved.

▌ Emphasise the loss and downside if things do not change.

▌ Challenge and confront the active blockers. They can infect the silent majority who are simply fearful or currently lack the necessary skills.

▌ Create a route map, providing a framework for the rationally minded as well as a psychological net of what's happening next.

▌ Encourage and build on islands of creativity.

▌ Communicate, communicate, communicate.

Typical approaches to harness innovation include:

▌ strategic creative methods that encourage thinking outside of existing mindsets

■ deep dive methods – such as that used by IDEO (they call it focused chaos) – that foster brainstorming and creativity

■ lateral thinking

■ open space, where all the stakeholders are in the room to find topics of traction.

Typical tools to increase collaboration include:

■ engagement strategies

■ stakeholder mapping and management

■ network analysis

■ identifying structural routines and psychological payoffs

■ non-participant observation

■ group analysis of the top team and intergroup dynamics as a micro-system.

Summary

■ To get people on board, managers need to understand the organisational culture and the personal journey that affects the individual responses to change.

■ Culture creates context. It is a function of the organisation's history, leadership – past and present – business context and performance.

■ There are types of organisations that are open to innovation and change. In these organisations, the context is able to excite and take people with them.

■ Some organisations favour inertia. Negative cultural dynamics operate under the surface of most systems that experience difficulties in change.

■ People have different responses to change depending upon their personal experiences, attachment styles and mindsets.

■ Most people appreciate help, engagement and respect. At the same time, be prepared to confront the minority of saboteurs and root them out.

7
How do you restructure for change?

Structure creates freedom.

Attributed to Erich Fromm

T he executive team of a corporate bank sat down at their annual offsite meeting to review the company's strategic performance. The financial figures were lacklustre – 10 per cent below headline target. The operational metrics had barely been met. Talent was poorly managed such that high performers were leaving during a period of intense market competition. Things were not looking good.

A dark cloud hung over the group – a team that already suffered from poor dynamics – as they thumbed through more and more depressing data. The tension in the room was palpable, heightened by a leader with a ruthless intellect that could shred any argument in a matter of seconds. No one dared to speak unless asked a direct question, and ideas were not aired or tested for fear of humiliation.

After a day of going through the reports, they agreed upon a key theme: the bank needed to sell more profitable business. This shared insight seemed to offer a temporary glow of satisfaction in a generally depressing series of sessions.

The competitive nature of retail banking meant that there was little scope for increasing market share. What the bank needed to do was to increase the wallet share of its existing and very loyal customer base. It needed to do more cross-selling. For example, when customers had extended overdrafts, was this an opportunity for a loan? Did the group have shared customer databases, or were they all doing their own thing? Could the bank recognise customers by segments and needs rather than by products?

The woeful answer to these questions was always negative. Connecting customer needs was by accident rather than by design. Each division had its own databases, built up over decades. Products were king. When I brought it to their attention that their collective interests were met by sharing data, the real differences began to emerge. One comment was that divisions ran and coded customers in different ways, so it was impossible to have a common database. Stories of recently implemented customer relationship management systems going wrong and not worth the cost and disruption were echoed by experiences in other banks. 'How do we know it'll provide the answers we are looking for?' cried the head of loans.

After listening to another round of reasons why this would not work, the group's managing director declared: 'This is nonsense.' He drilled down with laser logic to find the underlying reasons why working together was so hard. They eventually came out. Everyone liked the way the current structures were organised. Each division had its own fiefdom. They were accountable only to the managing director. They operated completely independently.

Structure as a framework

Structure provides the framework and environment for organisational health and performance. Max Weber's classic *Theory of Social and Economic Organisation* argues that bureaucracy helps to create consistency, reduces the vagaries of individual leaders, and provides clarity of roles and relationships. Weber counselled that managers be appointed on merit, skills and expertise rather than political favouritism. His notion of rational bureaucracy means that organisations should be based on functional specialisation, clear lines of hierarchical authority, expert training of managers, and decision making based on rules and tactics developed to guarantee consistent and effective pursuit of organisational goals. In essence, good structures facilitate organisational efficiency and stability. However, the word 'structure' is often associated with the negative side of bureaucracy, impeding options and stifling creativity. All too often, the result is groups reverting to organisational and structural silos.

Silos usually reflect that something in the organisational has gone wrong. Their presence reflects a localised solution to a system that functions poorly. While silos offer a great deal of personal flexibility and independence, they often mean duplication, difficulties across boundaries within the organisation, and structural rigidities that stop new ideas and innovation. When it comes to organisational change, the best way to stop anything happening is to cling to silos. So what type of organisational structures *does* work best for organisational change?

Driving change through restructuring

We know that structure follows strategy, and strategy is a response to market opportunities. So how do we get these things aligned? The simple answer is to drive change through restructuring.

Structural contingency theory argues that organisations' structures fit with environmental and strategic demands. Organisations that operate in stable environments are more likely to operate functional, centralised structures. These drive efficiencies and control. Organisations in dynamic and rapidly changing situations tend to do better with divisionalised, decentralised structures, where they are more responsive to market needs. A dynamic analysis of 262 large firms observed over 28 years generally supported the hypothesis, indicating a direct relationship between strategy and structure.[1] Furthermore, the results support the original conception of a hierarchical relationship between the two: strategy is a more important determinant of structure than structure is of strategy. Thus, understanding your organisational structure and how to manage it for change are essential for success.

[1] Amburgey, T. L. and Dacin, T. (1994) 'As the left foot follows the right? The dynamics of strategic and structural change', *Academy of Management*, December, 37, 6, pp.1427–52.

A do-or-die situation

For an American company, facing Chapter 11 – one step away from bankruptcy – is a sure way to get prepared for change. It is a do-or-die situation, and some may argue you have nothing to lose. It feels very different to those actually in the predicament, though – they have *everything* to lose: jobs, brand, the livelihood of hundreds, the end of a legacy.

Think of the US airline industry which has seen major changes over the past decades thanks to deregulation, low-cost carriers such as Southwest Airlines, and fierce competition from home and abroad. Pan Am, the first international airline and arguably the nation's flagship airline, went under, and in 2002 it looked as though the same was about to happen to United Airlines.

United, the second-largest US airline, invoked Chapter 11, imperilling its 85,000 employees worldwide. At the time of its bankruptcy filing, United was losing more than $7 million a day and facing nearly $1 billion in deferred debt obligations.

Chairman and CEO Glenn Tilton said at the time, 'We took the right decision to do today what is right for the company now,' and that he expected United to emerge as a different company tomorrow. He made the hard call of undertaking severe cuts in order to survive in the longer term.

The key to successful organisational change in this instance was in comprehensive restructuring and, in particular, focusing on the operational rigidities that led to high costs and poor use of assets, human and physical. It meant wide consultative discussions and involvement of all the major stakeholders. While consultation can take a long time, the pressure of Chapter 11 engendered a sense of purpose, clarity and urgency.

However, it was not an easy process. First, United's management needed to create a post-restructuring vision before they started. Their goal was to be not only a successful airline but one positioned to compete in the longer run. The directors set out a road map of the journey and rallied employees and stakeholders around this common strategic direction. It was not just a quick fix.

The sense of urgency meant that United could get the consultation process working quickly and smoothly, reducing wage costs in months rather than years. The group had a comprehensive restructuring exercise that broke down many of the silos, unravelled legacy practices, and tackled the problems of operational inefficiencies and high costs.[2] The buy-in from employees made it easier. Management was collectively able to break through these structural inefficiencies and save the company. Silos can kill change; restructuring is what can destroy them.

In 2006, a deal was struck to everyone's satisfaction, and United emerged from Chapter 11. The story shows how silos can really stop a company from realising its economic value. You do not have to wait until the bailiffs are at the door to do something about it. Clearly, United is an extreme case but it does show the dangers if the problem of structural rigidities go unchecked. The difference between those companies that can make change happen and those that cannot at the structural level is fluid execution.

What are the 'change qualities'?

Our research found that the companies high on change also had high levels of structural coherence. These were characterised by various qualities. It was easy for workflows to operate, connections and contact with other units and departments within the organisation were high, communication around tasks was easy, people were clear about their own roles and those of others, and silos were minimal. Companies that found it difficult to change complained of organisational silos, the barriers of working across units and the painfully slow pace of change. Both our research and the work of others underscore the importance of structural ease and how silo effects can wreck change efforts.[3]

A company need not be in crisis to gain the benefits of fluid execution. Some companies are hard-wired in that way.

[2] James H.M. 'Sprayregen', *Financial Executive*, June, pp.24–7.

[3] Hannan, M.T., Paolos, L. and Carroll, G.R (2006) 'The Fog of Change: Opacity and Aperity in Organisations', *Administrative Science Quarterly*, 48, pp.399–432; Prahalad, C.K. (2004) 'The Blinders of Dominant Logic', *Long Range Planning*, 37, pp.171–9.

Toyota's fluid execution

Toyota has a culture steeped in the philosophy of continuous change and process improvement; it is part of its organisational DNA and is inculcated into each worker through the company's five key principles of relentless improvement. The secret to Toyota's success of fluid execution success is founded upon five organisational processes:

1 *Kaizen* is the well-known Japanese process of continuous improvement. There is a belief that the company's front-line workers are a source of ideas and innovation for improvement and not just cogs in the endless manufacturing machine. Thus, there is good communication between the front line and managers.

2 *Genchi genbutsu* roughly translates as 'go to the source'. Workers are encouraged to find facts rather than relying on untested beliefs.

3 'Challenge' encourages Toyota employees to view problems positively. This has the objective of reframing, as discussed in Chapter 5 (pp. 63–5) on interpreting.

4 Teamwork, putting the higher goal first over self-interest. The collective interest is served, and thus people find ways to work better together rather than compete. It does not come easy. Toyota devotes a lot of time and money to on-the-job training and working better together, across boundaries.

5 Respect for other people is essential. There can be disagreement within the company, and this is seen as healthy. Toyota believes that if two people always agree then one of them is superfluous. It is not a company of 'yes' men and women.

These qualities make Toyota one of the world's leading car makers – and currently the largest – and why year after year it is recognised as one of the world's most innovative companies. These principles facilitate fluid execution and cohesive, facilitating structures, where goals, roles, boundaries, procedures and relationships are not left to chance.[4]

---

[4] *The Economist* (2006), 'Inculcating Culture', 21 January.

Structural relationships

How do you establish cohesive structures for fluid execution? Start with the design of the organisation at the macro level. We know that structure follows strategy and that the overall structure supports organisational goals.

Structure provides the framework for organisational work. It operates at several levels: roles and tasks, accountabilities and reporting lines, clusters of working relationships, and at the macro level of organisational design, where functions or geographies may be a sensible form of aligning activities.

Organisations set up structures to suit their needs. Henry Ford's focus on cost efficiencies and productivity meant that Ford was centralised, process-driven, and mechanistic during the growth period of the US car industry from the 1930s through to the 1960s. The idea was to meet the needs of the mass market and gain sales by volume and low pricing.

During the same period, General Motors sought actively to segment the market by customer needs, aspiration and income. So it produced cars with extra features to attract different segments. The company, originally a collection of rival car makers, established a multi-divisional structure, in which each division made a type of car for its own market, with its own production facility, marketing and internal services. With Ford and GM, two different structures met different strategic goals.

During periods of change, structural integration, free-flowing information and co-ordination are processes that help. However, within each organisation there is an inherent tension in balancing the needs of the whole organisational system against those of the organisational sub-units.

The resolution of these tensions can help or hinder the organisational sub-groups from attaining their objectives. The literature suggests that there are three states or outcomes that rise from this conflict.

State one

The first state is where the organisational needs, tasks and boundaries are supreme. The highest level of the organisational hierarchy sets the agenda of the sub-group, and there is no real differentiation between the wider systems and the group. Thus, the system is highly centralised, and the group is 'tightly coupled' to the wider system of the organisation. The sub-group fails to exert its own distinctiveness or identity independently. Theory suggests that this structural relationship reduces the impact of the sub-group, its task performance and creativity because its agenda is subsumed by the wider organisation. The benefits are that the whole system operates efficiently, roles are clear, and work gets done by control mechanisms. In stable environments, the organisation gains the economic advantages of consistency, efficiency benefits and exploiting a well-worn formula or recipe. But when the environment changes and becomes more turbulent, studies show, such companies tend to underperform their more nimble counterparts.[5]

CASE STUDY

US Steel

US Steel, during its long twentieth-century dominance, represents a typical centralised organisation. It owned and managed the whole process from extracting ore and coal from the ground, smelting, fashioning steel sheets, wires and slabs, to distribution. The company reaped economies of scale as well as market power.

State two

The second state is where the sub-group's agenda, task and boundaries are so distinct and separate that the group is disintegrated from the wider systems. The sub-group operates as a silo, with boundaries closed to the influence of its organisational context.

[5] Burns, T. and Stalker, G.M. (1961) *The Management of Innovation*, Tavistock, London; Emery, F.E. and Trist, E.L. (1965) 'The Causal Texture of Organisational Environments', *Human Relations*, 18, pp.21–31.

Theory suggests that sub-groups operating in this state will be less effective. Closed systems lack an external reference; they do not use the wider organisation's resources, ideas or networks. Closed biological systems tend to have a short life. In organisational settings, ideas, change and innovation are the casualties.

A local public-sector organisation

One of the study sites was a local, public-sector organisation, with a budget over £300 million and 8,000 employees. The formal organisational chart suggested that it was structured to gain efficiencies. The results for structural coherence showed very low scores and silo-behaviour tendencies. Further analysis of the data and a session with the top directors showed political backbiting, protection of budgets and active silos. These behaviours were damaging the reputation of the organisation and reducing efficiencies and quality services to the community. Silos kill initiative but make the hoarders feel better. It's a win-lose strategy with an overall impact that is invariably negative.

State three

The final state is where sub-groups are able to manage the tensions between being separate or distinctive as well as related and integrated with the wider organisational systems. Sub-groups that fulfill these conditions are described as 'loosely coupled'. They strike the balance between the internal and external management of their boundaries, negotiate task priorities or conflicts, and are able to mutually benefit from social and resource networks between the sub-group and the wider organisational system. Sub-groups that are loosely coupled tend to have greater impact and creativity. They have been described as organic, flexible, responsive and even ambidextrous. They have the advantages of responding to high levels of environmental change and creating varied internal structures that meet the complexities of the environment. These networked structures engender fluid execution.

Professional services firms such as McKinsey & Co. are good at working across organisational boundaries.

> **CASE STUDY**
>
> ## Morgan Stanley
>
> When John Mack took over at Morgan Stanley in 1993, he was shocked by the number of silos. He wanted to change both the culture and the way people were rewarded so that it operated as 'one firm'. Changing to structures that valued divisions' individual contributions as well as the collective power of them working together could be a force for change. Morgan Stanley's 'one firm' vision is intended to orient the firm to an increasingly complex, fast-paced global industry. The mission statement adds: 'We will distinguish ourselves by creating an environment that promotes teamwork and innovation.' Organic, matrixed and loosely coupled firms do better during externally driven change.

Breaking down silos

Organisations requiring change must cut down silos.

BBC director general Greg Dyke wanted to cut through the organisational dynamics that were impeding changes. He needed to get a grip of the organisation, slim down processes, increase the speed of decision making and align the organisation with its core purpose and focus. He launched a campaign to cut through all of the barriers and unhelpful legacies of the past.

Dyke wanted action. He would ask that people in every team in the BBC to discuss how to make the place better, how to make it exciting and how to overcome the cynics and moaners in the organisation. Dyke exhorted his people to 'cut the crap and make it happen'. His role was that of an agent provocateur. He was not responsible for every change; neither was that possible. Rather, he provoked change by creating the conditions for people to do more for themselves. In a slightly chaotic world, people were themselves the agents of change.

We know that positive internal networks are a powerful way to assist organisations to change. People who command social capital and work with different groups attract others around them to form important node points or connections within the organisation, linkages and hubs in the social network.[6] They can help facilitate flow, information, resources, political favour and change. Social network theory tells us that they can be a real advantage. These same people can, however, also be a point of blockage.

What needs to be done in your organisation?

You do not have to be running the BBC, United Airlines or Morgan Stanley to understand what needs to be done in your organisation.

How were your scores on fluid execution? You may recall when you filled in the questionnaire (see Appendix 2 or visit the full version at www.ilyasjarrett.com) that structure can create inertia or deliver a superior speed of execution. Was it hard or easy to do business across the organisation? Were you bureaucratic or organic? Was it hard to spawn new structures that enabled change, or were such initiatives met with co-operation?

Low scorers will reinforce any cultural tendencies to keep things the same. They remain safe in structural rigidities and the comfort of the familiar – in which case there is cause for concern and urgent action. It will certainly slow down change capability. Companies that have higher scores will find change easier to make; they demonstrate greater fluidity and are more likely to respond quickly.

What can managers do?

▌ Align your structure to your strategy. Do you know what your business strategy is? Do you have a simple business model that you understand and can communicate to your people?

[6] See the importance of networking in Uzzi, B. and Dunlap, S. (2005) 'How to Build Your Network', *Harvard Business Review*, December, pp.1–8; Tsai, W. and Ghoshal, S. (1998) 'Social Capital and Value Creation: the role of intrafirm networks', *Academy of Management Journal*, 41, 4, pp.464–76; and Burt, R. (1992) *Structural Holes: The Social Structure of Competition*, Harvard University Press, Cambridge, MA.

▌ Given that, what are you trying to achieve? Better co-ordination, better workflows, process management across boundaries, better intergroup relations, and a reduction of overlap and role confusion.

▌ Understand the underlying structural tendencies in your business. Is it centralised, loosely coupled or siloed with the rest of the organisation?

▌ Align divisions' macro structure to the needs of the environment.

▌ Where organisations are operating in a strategic context that is more stable, honing advantages from consistency should be sought.

▌ Incremental process or structural changes can be developed, but be aware that the advantages may be short-lived.

▌ However, for the majority of companies, change will be required in some part of the structure, be it at a macro level (such as the whole business unit) or a micro level such as a division or department.

▌ Thus, a restructuring exercise is required.

▌ The level of structural change is at the highest level of influence that you have as a manager. You should be looking up to see what's happening at levels above you.

▌ Fast-moving environments need structures that are loosely coupled and networked. The focus of the change will determine the details of what will take place.

▌ Typical responses:

  – *to poor workflow* may be process innovation and redefining the process chain

  – *to confusion about role and authority* is working through the RACI method of collectively clarifying among the stakeholders who is *responsible*, who has *authority*, where do you need to *consult*, and who needs to be *informed*.

  – *to poor intergroup relations* is working through the root causes of the problems in an open forum and committing to action groups for resolution.

  – *to silos* is to break these up through structural devices so that new work groups are formed, new roles specified and patterns of work are changed as well.

■ Structural changes must be socialised in order to be successful. Thus, the case and benefits for change need to be made in terms that people can answer the question: 'What does it mean for me?'

■ Engagement strategies that get buy-in from internal and external stakeholders mean that the legacy issues do not simply go to ground. Thus, running focus groups, forums, training programmes and town-hall meetings will be all part of the mix of activities that are required to make the benefits of structural change a reality.

Typical tools and techniques:

■ pilot projects

■ cross-functional/work streams and tiger teams

■ RACI

■ managing the matrix

■ organisational design

■ business process re-engineering

■ supply-chain management.

Summary

■ Structure follows strategy and is a critical device in organising for change.

■ Structural inertia halts the process of successful change.

■ Organisations that have deep silos make the transition and communication of new ideas, practices and behaviours hard to implement.

■ All organisations have to manage the tension of meeting the needs of the sub-unit as well as the wider organisation. Successful ones create cohesive structures.

■ Organisations with loosely coupled structures that are interconnected and organic are associated with change.

■ People's need for clarity can be met with thoughtful engagement strategies.

part

Developing strategies for change

Part 3 of the book puts the discussion of internal capabilities in Part 2 into context. Identifying and building these capabilities is necessary but insufficient. We also need to relate them to the outside world, which can be predictable and stable, or turbulent and unrelenting. Each combination of internal capabilities can be matched to the external conditions. Four generic strategies can help managers increase their rate of successful change based on their changeability ratings.

▌ Zone one is the *steady state*.

▌ Zone two is the *risk zone*.

▌ Zone three is the *comfort zone*.

▌ Zone four is the *Zen zone*.

Together, these four outcomes or zones of change imply different strategies for change.[1] And they provide managers with some choices.

---

[1] A number of cases in Part 3 arise directly from our research. Thus, company identities have had to be disguised to maintain anonymity.

The following chapters explain each zone and their features so that you can recognise them easily. They offer business cases of how companies have thrived, survived and died, based on our research and consulting engagements. Each chapter concludes with tips and hints on what managers can do.

Overall summary of strategic choices[2]

Zones	Adaptive strategies for change	Characteristics of strategy	Risks or negative outcomes
Steady state	'Conforming' – builds on existing recipe of competence	Developing stability, incremental change, process improvements	Compliance, rituals and excessive controls lead to ineffective bureaucracy and rigidity
Risk	'Reforming' or turnaround – ripping up the old and dictating the new	Punctuated change: rapid, focused and 'aggressive'	It is only a temporary excursion, default to old ways and potential for failure and demise; high risks
Comfort	'Deforming' – redefining or reframing through values and behaviours – sails full out	Need to create disconfirming reality and challenge current paradigms and assumptions; engage and involve key stakeholders	Complacency and lose competitive advantage/edge
Zen	'Transforming' – moving from an oil tanker to a fleet of sailing dinghies!	Strategically orientated change that impacts on culture and structure	Change junkie sees activity as more important than insightful change

2 See also Appendix 5.

8 Reap from steady state

Good design is good business.

Thomas J. Watson, president of IBM

In the 1993 comedy *Groundhog Day*, Bill Murray plays a TV weatherman trudging off to remote Punxsutawney, Pennsylvania, to cover the annual 2 February festival.[1] The next morning, he awakes to discover that it's 2 February again. And again. He tries to break the pattern, through pranks, subversion, and even, eventually, suicide attempts, but nothing changes.

So Murray's trapped weatherman embraces his fate. As the weeks tick by, each day he learns something new about the characters around him in the town and discovers how he can make Punxsutawney a better place.

Groundhog Day holds a deep moral about the importance of meaningful relationships and self-discovery. But perhaps a more important lesson is how the film – in highlighting the slow and deliberate nature of both time and space – serves as an exaggerated example of an environment in steady state. Change, at best, is incremental.

[1] Groundhog Day is a holiday celebrated in the United States and Canada on 2 February. Traditionally, it is the day the groundhog emerges from his hole after a long winter's hibernation. If it sees its shadow, it regards the shadow as an omen of six more weeks of bad weather and returns to its hole. If it's cloudy and hence no shadow, the groundhog takes it as a sign of spring and stays above ground.

The frustrating nature of such a state is obvious, and those familiar with the film experience these moments along with a range of other emotions. Steady state has its advantages, though. In particular, a stable environment provides predictability and certainty; the tramlines of life are clear. Organisations can gain better efficiencies and tend to be more dependable. We can gain the most from what we know. This chapter looks at organisations that exist in an environment of steady state and the implications for change.

What is the steady state zone?

Zone one is described as 'steady state'. It is characterised by a placid, slow-paced or predictable environment; it becomes a highly structured context. It is matched internally by protracted and deliberate decision making, and bounded by long-standing conventions. These conditions originate from little, if any, environmental change and low, internal, strategic capacity to change. Here, organisations are likely to be in steady-state worlds, and there is consistency between the inner world and the external reality. This zone tends to be dominated by companies that prefer incremental change initiatives which yield low benefits in terms of performance. The company finds a segment or operates in a structured market where things do not radically change.

The opportunities here are that the organisation increases its efficiency, exploits its learning, and builds up a greater and deeper learning specialisation in order to do things even better.[2] However, there is also a danger of complacency through what has been dubbed the 'competency trap' and organisational capability declining to 'core rigidity'. The recipe for success becomes a potential stumbling block.[3]

[2] Benner, M.J. and Tushman, M.L. (2003) 'Exploitation, Exploration and Process Management: the productivity dilemma revisited', *Academy of Management Review*, 28, 2, pp.238–56; and March, J.G. (1991) 'Exploration and Exploitation in Organisational Learning', *Organisation Science*, 2, 1, pp.71–87.

[3] The dangers of the 'competency trap' and core competencies becoming 'core rigidities' are discussed respectively by Levitt, B. and March, J. (1988) 'Organisational Learning', *Annual Review of Sociology*, 14, pp.319–40; and Leonard-Barton, D. (1992) 'Core capabilities and core rigidities: A Paradox in Managing New Product Development', *Strategic Management Journal*, 13, pp.111–125.

A competency trap or core rigidity comes from a company being successful in its core practices or operations. These core competencies or excellent practices become a source of competitive advantage. Thus, companies get really good at something and decide that this is the recipe for future gain. They specialise, fine-tune and invest energy, time and resources to perfect their methodology. But then the environment changes, or competitors see what to do and imitate.

EXAMPLE

Chrysler's core competency

In the 1980s, Chrysler led the automotive field in minivans. It practically invented them. The company's innovations and investments focused on improving production techniques and variations on the minivan. Then suddenly, things changed. SUVs came on the scene. Consumer tastes changed. More and more competitors entered the minivan market. Chrysler had few strategies to meet these threats. The company was tied into its existing legacy of competencies, shackled by an inability to change. The crisis deepened, threatening Chrysler's very survival, and the one-time industrial giant accepted an inferior position in a 'merger' with Daimler-Benz. Chrysler's core competency became its Achilles heel.

My view is that executives have choices. If they recognise the five factors laid out in Part 2, some of the traps can be avoided.

How does a company know it is in this zone? Consider the situation of the Regional Development Fund (RDF). It may appear an extreme case to make the point, but if any of it sounds familiar, then it may apply to your organisation.

The Regional Development Fund

The RDF was set up in 1975 to meet charitable and development needs in emergent economies. The RDF was underpinned by strong values and a clear mission statement of meeting the needs of a specific target group; it had donors from a number of rich countries.

Indeed, funding was ample, and the RDF was fortunate to operate in an environment of low pressure. The organisation had been able to grow each year without additional demands.

Inside, though, the situation was less rosy. The strategic leadership was introspective, low on both scanning and insights based on the Changeability questionnaire. There had been very little turnover at the top of the organisation for a decade, and middle managers saw the leadership group as removed or even out of touch. The leadership group also saw the organisation's health significantly more positively than middle managers. To further complicate the situation, the top management team lacked an organisational strategy, an external perspective and the energy to do anything different. The RDF's success rested on a great track record, they argued. Why change anything?

The organisation was characterised by a defended culture. Examples of dysfunctional routines are shown in 'never deliver bad news', 'the boss is always right', and high levels of dysfunctional political behaviours. Over a third of managers saw the culture as 'too bureaucratic'.

These problems were made more difficult by the organisation being centrally controlled. Management issued directives that staff were expected to follow to the letter. And while one might expect high degrees of bureaucratic efficiency, the RDF's culture seemed to resist the advantages of centralisation. Decision making and actions were protracted and often poorly implemented. It could take several weeks to get a decision on a simple request concerning a minor expenditure or policy recommendation. The organisation's excessive formality and hierarchical nature was apparent in its high score on silo effects, a lack of co-operation across departments and poor information flow. While the agency continued to attract funds, its cost-to-distribution ratio was well above international benchmarks.

RDF lacked the appetite for change, a fact reflected in its low change-index score. If the organisation had any change strategy at all, it was a 'conforming strategy' of 'cultural development' marked by the desire to remain consistent with existing practice. The aim: to maintain the cultural mores, the norms of the organisation, stability and an efficient distribution channel. But it still failed to fully realise the benefits of its current situation. What could be done to make change happen? (See page 119.)

What are the strategies for change in a steady state zone?

From a corporate-citizenship angle, McDonald's is an unlikely model for a business book to recommend emulating. Critics have long attacked its sodium- and fat-heavy menus, and the company has been a frequent target of anti-globalisation and environmental protestors and a whipping boy of anti-American sentiment. It has struggled, particularly in Europe, with hostile media coverage and has been forced to defend itself in high-profile lawsuits. The documentary *Super Size Me* made plain the potential ill effects of a McDonald's-based diet. The company managed to hit No. 48 in the 2007 *BusinessWeek*–Boston Consulting Group World's 50 Most Innovative Companies report, but it showed a big fat zero in the patent citation index. There's the occasional launch of a new menu item, but few see McDonald's as a wild innovator. So, what do corporate change seekers have to learn from such a company?

In early 2008, CEO Jim Skinner commented:

> 'McDonald's consolidated performance continues to reflect our enduring profitable growth with comparable sales up 6.8 per cent for the year – one of our strongest increases since the initiation of our Plan to Win. We continue to drive our business by linking consumer insights to our strategies of convenience, branded affordability and innovative menu offerings.'

McDonald's reported the following fourth-quarter highlights:

▌Global comparable sales increased 6.7 per cent, after a 6.3 per cent increase in 2006.

▌Growth in consolidated company-operated and franchised restaurant margins for the eighth consecutive quarter.

▌Consolidated operating income increased 22 per cent.

For the full year 2007, McDonald's revenues reached a record high of $22.8 billion, with global sales up 6.8 per cent. In short, something is going on that works. Behind the controversies and hyperbole, one must wonder: how does McDonald's continue, after decades on top, to show such strong growth without dramatic innovation?

McDonald's operates in a highly competitive but stable market, filled with the likes of Burger King and Kentucky Fried Chicken. It should be no surprise that burgers provide the lion's share of revenue, supplemented by various types of chicken sandwiches and products, French fries, soft drinks, breakfast items and desserts. In most markets, McDonald's offers salads and vegetarian items, wraps and, sometimes, localised fare. The chain is particularly known for this regional deviation from the standard menu, one employed either to abide by regional food customs and practices (such as the religious prohibition of beef consumption in India) or to make available foods with which the regional market is more familiar (such as the sale of McRice in Indonesia). Overall, McDonald's does not aim to draw in customers with a wide range of products. Its response to change is incremental as players battle for market share among the fast-food contenders.

Founded in 1948, McDonald's underwent a fundamental makeover at the hands of new owner Ray Kroc in 1955. Kroc codified key operational elements, from buying to frying, and developed a system to make burgers consistently. This set of instructions became the manual that franchises used to 'manage' the system. This dominant logic and structural procedures still make the company work. They are a large part of the McDonald's DNA – and of its success.

One of the secrets behind the company is that it has used the same efficiency-based business model for over 50 years, aiming:

▌ to have an instantly recognisable brand

▌ to offer popular, consistent-tasting meals

▌ to serve them quickly

▌ to sell them at posted and stable prices

▌ to create a eye-catching, colourful, circus-like atmosphere that is consistent to every restaurant

▌ to have independent, franchised locations throughout the country (now throughout the world) so there is always one near you.

The company serves approximately 56 million customers every day at 31,000 stores in 120 territories. Operating in a relatively stable market, McDonald's thrives by taking advantage of incremental change.

The operations, wielding massive buying power efficiently, focus on lean manufacturing. There are comparatively few choices when it comes to the question of change. So marketing, new menus and how franchises use their space are everything.

For example, in 2005 the company pushed franchisees to consider making their restaurants 24/7, thereby tapping a new market of shift workers and early risers. In Garner, North Carolina, franchise owner Fred Huebner catered to the area's 'night owls and early birds' – and increased his restaurant's revenue by 4.5 per cent in its first 18 months. 'There are so many customers out there all times of the day,' he told *Business Week*. 'We have to be out there, too.'[4]

Denis Hennequin took over as president of the slumping McDonald's Europe in 2005. His solution to reviving sales was not radical: he focused on fine-tuning the Big Mac way to be 'locally relevant' and improve the experience of visiting the 6,400 restaurants under his umbrella.

Hennequin adopted some simple rules that seemed to make a difference. He introduced an 'open door' visitor day so that the

---

[4] *Business Week* (2007) 'McDonald's 24/7', 5 February. By focusing on the hours between traditional mealtimes, the fast-food giant is sizzling.

company was more transparent and allowed a space for customers to express concerns about local practices. As part of the local focus, McDonald's Europe prefers to hire managers from the area. It buys locally so that it is part of the local economy and the supply chain can be well managed. Four-fifths of its supplies in France come from local farmers, for example. (Some of the French farmers who campaigned against the company in the late 1990s subsequently discovered that it was, in fact, buying their produce.)[5] The company also provides ever more information to its customers about the content and ingredients of its food – which, of course, varies as little as possible from restaurant to restaurant.

The market has seen growth over the decades. However, its structure has remained fairly stable over the years as rivalry among dominant players keeps margins and market share keen. The key lesson in operating in this zone from McDonald's is that the company has utilised the same business model and operational framework since it was established. Management has driven the same dominant logic and seen efficiencies as the main way of creating value. Changes, almost invariably incremental in scale, have extended the basic formula.

Organisations in the steady state can profit from their situation. It means that they have the ability to reap the benefits of efficiency, consistency and predictability.

The imperatives for change tend to be simple: maintain revenue streams, margins and market share. The strategy for change is to keep fit and stay trim; the approach will be characterised by incremental and process changes. This means fine-tuning things that are working and making slight adjustments to things that need fixing.

Companies adopting this approach of conforming to their existing model of working would tend to maintain industry 'best practice', making process improvements in their core technology. One would not see a radical change in strategy or culture.

[5] *The Economist* (2007) 'Happy meal: How a Frenchman is reviving McDonald's in Europe', 25 January.

The dangers of steady state

Dell is another company that typifies this model. Steady state provides many advantages but it can also lead to becoming stuck in a rut. Once a leader in introducing low-cost personal computers, it has found new sources of competition. The growth of the PC market is approaching maturity. Worldwide PC shipments have grown approximately 12 per cent a year – much better than expected. Yet small compared to 1990s when growth rates were twice that amount. In 2008, it is estimated that PCs will reach a high of 260 million with emerging markets fuelling the drive.[6]

Dell's strategic response in terms of change has tended to exploit its original entry strategy by continual striving for process improvements. The company originally took on the computer industry by offering computers faster, cheaper and more fully loaded than anyone else – and more easily customisable. On release, Dell computers were 40 per cent cheaper than IBM's, with units delivered in a few days. (I can attest to this myself, having bought three over the years.) The Shannon facility in Ireland used to boast that it could make up a Dell machine to order within half an hour. It's probably faster now.

Finally, Dell still offers enhancements at half the cost of major competitors. The operating model emphasises mass customisation and no-nonsense service. Dell has not done too badly from this approach. In 2006, *Fortune* listed Dell as the 25th-largest US company as well as the 8th most-admired company. In 2007, Dell ranked 34th and 8th, respectively. A 2006 publication identified Dell as 1 of 38 companies in the S&P 500 that had consistently outperformed the market over the previous 15 years.[7]

But the trend did not last. The environment contested Dell's position with unexpected changes. Competitors were able to match

[6] *The Economist* (2007) 'Personal computers, There's life in the old dog yet', 30 August.

[7] See *Dell at a Glance – Company Facts*; and Frigo, M.L., Needles, B.E. and Powers, P. (2006) 'Strategy and Integrated Financial Ratio Performance Measures: Further Evidence of the Financial Performance Scorecard and High Performance Companies', *Studies in Managerial and Financial Accounting*, 16.

low prices. Emerging markets grew faster but were not socialised nor had access to online purchasing. More power and frills were no longer persuasive extras – most competitors could easily match these features. Internally, Dell also shot itself in the foot. A recall of 4 million computers due to faulty 'flaming batteries' – an external dependency from suppliers – plus accounting irregularities, meant Dell had to restate its profits. Dell also found itself second to HP and losing market share and growth (see Figure 8.1).

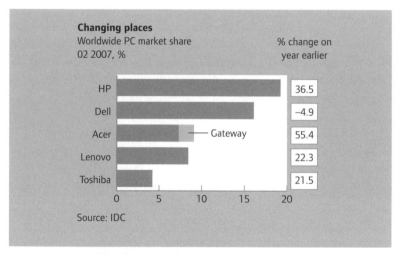

FIGURE 8.1 Worldwide PC market share

To shake things up, founder Michael Dell resumed his role as CEO and chairman in January 2007. At the executive level, the company swept out a number of key figures, bringing in appointees from outside the computer industry – a formidable group with a fresh perspective at the strategic apex of the organisation. Michael Dell admits that the 'monolithic model' of managing the supply chain has to change. It is no longer a recipe for success on its own. The company has set up a social networking space, IdeaStorm, to canvass and get input from customers. Seeing the world from the external view rather than internally is a cultural change for Dell. Even successful companies need to change before traps become derailers.

So how can managers implement this sort of change in the steady state zone?

The Regional Development Fund (continued)

Earlier, we saw the conflicts faced by the RDF. It characterises for me the issues of those organisations in the steady state zone. As you may recall, the RDF had a low adaptability to change. Its operating practices stumbled; its organisational effectiveness lagged.

You might say: let us start with scanning the external environment and protect against the dangers of external shocks. However, as you may recall, the RDF's top management group did not see that as a priority. A direct attempt to make changes within the leadership group would have been futile. The leader's long tenure, personal networks and reputation marked a symbol of safety, reliability and stability – exactly what donors wanted. Moreover, there were no immediate threats from the external environment – no 'competitors' for resources and growing donations year after year. It is difficult to create a sense of urgency under such conditions!

The focus of our support with this organisation was helping them work more efficiently and effectively and build up their internal capabilities. The results from the SCi questionnaire gave some initial clues on the main areas of concern: the RDF operated in silos, with schisms dividing sub-groups and manifesting itself in protectionism and office politics. These chains of the past had to be severed in order for the group to break through these inherent internal difficulties.

The RDF needed to be more internally connected. It would increase efficiencies, reduce administrative waste and duplication, and work to spend more of its donated dollars on the intended recipients: not-for-profit organisations and community groups.

Initial feedback from the survey and discussions did not surprise mid-tier managers, but the senior management saw the situation in rosier terms, and its data showed a much more favourable vision of the organisation than the rest of the organisation's.[8] We sought an intervention that would meet the needs of the organisation yet not lead to a total shutdown by senior management.

[8] Our research found that top levels of management consistently see the world more favourably than their mid-tier counterparts.

We designed a series of open, facilitated workshops to share the feedback and see what people wanted to do about making the organisation more efficient. Approximately 60 people attended these initial forums. Each had three parts:

1 Here's what the data says – what is your reaction?

2 Do you agree with the results?

3 Do they make sense to you?

The next phase was to help each of the groups define key priorities. Some simple criteria were set to help narrow down options. These included: level of impact, what resources would be required, whether senior management was likely to block it, and how feasible it would be to execute in six to nine months.

The groups eventually selected four projects for senior management agreement. Each laid out clear recommendations and corresponding benefits. Two passed, two deferred. Knowledge management and private-sector relationships met with senior management's approval. Each project set up a cross-group task team to take on the job of consulting, designing and piloting projects in these two areas.

Both projects took off and everyone was pleased. But, more importantly, these two projects laid down the foundations for similar initiatives over the years that followed. The organisation gained great benefits from these small initiatives beyond what it imagined.

The RDF first broke down some of the silos and poor intergroup relations by working in cross-functional teams on a common agenda. Barriers and stereotypes about each other came down. The organisation become more efficient and improved its ratio of costs to delivery by 20 per cent – still above international benchmarks – but a significant leap in the right direction nonetheless. These initiatives also helped shift the work climate and the relationships among the employees. The RDF became a place where ideas and initiatives could be considered rather than stamped on at birth. The programme's success shows how small, focused changes can have a huge impact and must not be underestimated.

At RDF, the leadership stayed intact, but the operating systems worked considerably better. People shared information more readily, workflows improved and decision making was quicker. I understand that similar workshops continue at RDF on an annual basis.

Pros and cons

The implications of this strategic response bring hope to managers at any level of the organisation:

▌ The steady state zone brings enormous benefits to a company because it provides consistency, stability and reliability. Its value is that it exploits existing assets, implicit knowledge, practices, and routines.

▌ It means that not every company needs to engage in radical change and that incrementalism is a legitimate strategy for change. We know from research that incremental changes tend to be more successful.

▌ It means that managers can do something to make a difference at the local level. Small process improvements can deliver differences to the bottom line.

However, this strategic response also has some drawbacks and pitfalls to avoid:

▌ Unexpected changes in the environment can wreak havoc on this type of strategic response and type of change. The Dell case highlights some of the dangers when competitors erode your market and profits.

▌ The benefits are modest; critics might say insubstantial.

▌ It may collude with poor practices or complacency in which organisational dominant logic inhibits any change at all.

Thus, managers need to take the benefits of 'keeping trim' and guard against the dangers. How can they do it?

Three main areas for attention

Managers must continue to build internal capability. This is a basic minimum for all companies. However, they should pay particular attention to three areas:

1 **Scanning the environment:** being taken unawares by sudden changes in the environment is the real danger in adopting this conformist strategy. This may be deregulation, new legislation or a new competitor. Leaders of organisations need to be vigilantly scanning their context for new trends and subtle changes. Is your organisation more like RDF or Procter & Gamble?

2 **Breaking down dominant logic:** efficiency and consistency create a mindset that can easily become reality. Assumptions go unchallenged, and core competencies become core rigidities. Taking things for granted about the industry or about the organisation may be examples. 'We have seen it before' or 'we always do that way' are phrases that should alert the antennae that complacency may be just around the corner. Managers need to avoid this trap. They should actively bring in outsiders – consultants or specialists in the short term, new leaders in the longer term. Michael Dell did exactly that when he changed most of his senior team in an effort to overcome the company's malaise.

3 Dominant logic is also challenged in **attacking the cultural norms, practices and behaviours**. Organisational rituals and symbols can be changed, from altering the working environment to more fundamental change in work groups.

Zone	Adaptive strategies for change	Characteristics of strategy	Risks or negative outcomes
Steady state	'Conforming' – builds on existing recipe of competence	Developing stability, incremental change, process improvements	Compliance, rituals and excessive controls lead to ineffective bureaucracy and rigidity

Summary

▌ It is heartening to find that organisations can locate a point of alignment – in this case, the steady state zone – between their internal readiness and the external environment.

▌ Steady state offers considerable advantages: efficiency, consistency and stability.

▌ Strategies for change in this situation will tend to be incremental and yield the benefits of efficiency and consistency. This is a perfectly respectable strategy and not all organisations have to do radical turnarounds to gain the benefits of change.

▌ Such an approach exploits the company's implicit capabilities and releases managers to manage.

▌ There are some pitfalls. Building active steps to stay aware of these can avoid the dangers of complacency and the competency trap.

9

Turnaround in the risk zone

For every thing there is a season. . . a time to weep, and a time to laugh; a time to mourn and a time to dance. . .

A time to get, and a time to lose; a time to keep and a time to cast away.

Ecclesiastes, 3: 1–6

The risk zone is turbulent, uncomfortable and the result of a misalignment between the demands of a fast-changing environment and the inability of an organisation to change.

Let's begin by looking at how a small reinsurance company suddenly found itself in the risk zone.

Finding yourself in the risk zone

The attacks of September 11, 2001, shocked the entire world morally and financially. Its toll on our lives – even those on different shores – was barely compensated, if at all. Reinsurance companies should have been the backstop in restoring financial stability, but the old rules didn't seem to apply in the face of new challenges, and the reinsurance industry found itself in as much turmoil as everyone else.

The biggest names in the reinsurance industry – Swiss Re, Munich Re, AIG – managed to muddle through, but many of the smaller operators went to the wall. One of these, on the brink of disaster, was Copenhagen Re, an 86-year-old stalwart. The events of 9/11 brought it to its knees. The huge wave of change hit the bow of this small boat, and the calls of 'Mayday' echoed across the market.

Søren Boe Mortensen, chief general manager of parent company Alm Brand Ltd, announced in an open letter to the Copenhagen Stock Exchange that Copenhagen Re had produced a loss of DKK 1,484 million (approx. £148m in 2008), largely due to the terrorist attack on the World Trade Center.[1] Management moved swiftly to make sizeable staff cuts, to restructure business, to slash costs and operations, and to stop taking on any more new business. It was a dent to national pride, and the company salvaged whatever honour it could by protecting the equity in the company and honouring existing liabilities. Management decided to 'run off' the business until all debts were settled, sold off and commitments had run their course. This could be as long as 20 years.

The market's response was predictable. Standard & Poor, an independent credit rating agency, dropped the company's investment rating from A- to BB, which means S&P viewed the company with less confidence. Things looked grim.

In the midst of these difficulties, an unexpected heroine arose. In November 2001, Anne Mette Barfod became CEO of Copenhagen Re. She had grown up in the industry as a pricing actuary, worked her way steadily through the organisation, and was now a member of the senior management group. The new order required someone open to change and capable of challenging existing norms and ways of working, while at the same time working to understand the organisation's long traditions and veteran workers.

The management team were told to sort it out. They selected Barfod to lead it. She had all the qualities of the change agent: she was clear about the goals, had depth of credibility and industry experience, understood how the internal dynamics of the company worked, and possessed strong interpersonal and communication skills. (See more about leading change in Part 4.) Her first reaction was to reject the role, but her colleagues all felt that she had

---

[1] Søren Boe Mortensen, letter to the Copenhagen Stock Exchange, 6 March 2002, pp.1–3.

something more to contribute – and suspected that they did not want to be managed by other members of the group. A consensus was reached, and reluctantly, she decided to take up the challenge.

Her intuition told her that people wanted more information, clarity of direction and communication. In the space of a few weeks, she had organised public consultations and meetings across the two main offices in Copenhagen and London. These were held in small groups so that people could talk about their real concerns, unburden themselves, and provide a chance for her to listen to their anxieties and fears. Having worked her way up the ranks, Barfod was able to relate to rank-and-file workers, and she was seen as approachable and genuinely interested in employees' comments. She was exactly what the employees needed during this period of turmoil. Managing the emotional turmoil and transition of change proved one of her key skills.

Listening had to be combined with additional leadership skills. Barfod's passion for the business and belief in the strategy of 'exit with dignity' was a mental strap line. She needed to get people engaged and willing to work in an environment that was in crisis. How do you get people motivated when there is no pot of gold at the end? She found a variety of ways – social events, individual recognition, sincere praise – to get people to carry on knowing that they would not necessarily have a job at the end. (We saw the importance of emotional security and transitions in Chapter 6.)

On a more strategic platform, she appealed to the greater purpose of the company's mission, values and pride. National pride was a rallying call. The higher values of doing a good job, never failing customers and leaving with dignity were part of the company's culture and psychological contract. She was able to tap into the group's shared and collective consciousness. (These methods smoothed the transition of change we discussed in Chapter 6).

The restructuring of processes to increase efficiencies in the administrative procedures and both offices being reorganised led to costs being slashed. The loss of staff and reduction in overheads by moving to a smaller London office and efficiencies meant considerable saving. And given there was no more new business, the economic model was to keep costs lower than existing investment income, package liabilities in a way that could be sold back to the original customers, and maintain a decent return on assets. Copenhagen Re moved from a colossal loss to break-even point in a few years.

With, at last, stability in the workforce, the company's solvency margin inched up marginally. Barfod had managed to steer a steady course for a company that was in dire straits and turn it away from bankruptcy.

When asked what made the difference, she replied:

> 'It was really difficult. Once we got through the first few months [late 2001] and listened to everyone, things got better. We had a plan. We then executed it with laser focus. But I always kept channels of communication open. I also really believed what we were doing was right for our people, the company, and our clients.'

Copenhagen Re was in what I call the 'risk' zone, so called because there is a likelihood of organisational derailment. It highlights the conditions where the environment is rapidly changing or turbulent while the organisational strategic change capability is low. There is a misalignment between the internal and external worlds. The likelihood is that organisations in this zone will experience crisis and lower performance as they lag behind competitors and threatening new entrants.[2] There may also be a risk of selection failure as environmental factors 'crowd out' internal capability. Some organisations that are able to learn from the changes can avoid failure.[3] However, this is not the norm.

---

[2] Ruef, M. (1997) 'Assessing Organizational Fitness on a Dynamic Landscape: An Empirical Test of the Relative Inertia Thesis', *Strategic Management Journal*, 18 pp.837–58. His study of over 600 hospitals concluded that inertia would tend to be negatively influenced by jolts in the external environment. Nelson, R.R. (1991) 'Why do Firms Differ, and How Does it Matter?', *Strategic Management Journal*, 12 pp.61–74, recognises how internal dynamic can help make a difference as does Boeker, W. (1997) 'Strategic Change: The Influence of Managerial Characteristics and Organisational Growth', 40, 1, pp.152–70, who shows the role of managerial capabilities.

[3] See Hannan, M.T., Paolos, L. and Carroll, G.R. (2003) 'The Fog of Change: Opacity and Aperity in Organizations', *Administrative Science Quarterly*, 48 pp.399–432: and Haverman, H.A. (1992) 'Between a Rock and a Hard Place: Organizational Change and Performance under Conditions of Fundamental Environmental Transformation', *Administrative Science Quarterly*, 37, pp.48–75.

Lessons learned

The case of Copenhagen Re highlights a number of lessons.

▌ Shocks come from unexpected places.

▌ The change strategy follows the organisational strategy.

▌ The fast pace of the external environment requires an equal response in the internal organisation to gain some level of alignment.

▌ Barfod's leadership style provided a clear differentiator and shows how a turnaround can be achieved with dignity and involvement.

Public-sector organisations face similar difficulties in bringing about change. 'Public Authority', a local authority, illustrates some of the challenges it faced in providing the full range of social services, social housing, infrastructure maintenance and environmental planning and health.

CASE STUDY

Public Authority

This was an organisation that served one of the poorest areas of the UK.

Public Authority operated in a highly regulated and technical environment. State government had identified the organisation as having a poor performance. It had gained a reputation for failing to meet budgetary targets, serving its local population, and had generated unfavourable headlines within the press for inefficiencies and poor practice. There were also disgruntled consumers and low staff morale according to external survey data. The pressure from its local politicians, the public and central government was increasing. The CEO was sacked and a new one stepped into the role.

Data from 64 senior managers saw the strategic leadership as introspective. They were low in both scanning and insights. The culture was seen as defensive and managers also reported 'a culture of fear'. This tone was also exacerbated by the organisation's long-service employee culture, where whole families across generations worked there. There were also cliques with an 'us' and 'them' divide across grades and tenure. (I was at a meeting among the managers where each was asking the other how long they had been there. 'Six years,' said one proudly. 'You're only a youngster,' came the reply.)

Public Authority's strategic ability to change was low and its performance assessment from national government statistics matched. It was at risk of derailment. An added dimension was the political dynamics of the elected officials.

The new CEO quickly grasped the difficulty of the situation and initiated a 'reforming' turnaround strategy. It involved a focus on performance in the worse areas, removing senior managers that were not performing, generating a sense of urgency and action on value-enhancing activities. The CEO spent endless hours and evenings attending committee meetings and managing the complex array of political stakeholders to get them on board for the changes. In addition, it was difficult to introduce high-performance standards in a culture that was unionised, socially homogenous where generations and extended family members could actual manage each other, and where long traditions held sway over new management practices.

Over 18 months of stress and hard work, the CEO saw the organisation's performance rating increase. It was almost at the cost of executive burnout. The CEO started with energy and focus but was so worn out by the end of the changes that he had to take extended leave. However, the danger of 'resting on laurels' always remained in the background. Such strategies of change need ongoing dedication.

Such changes are commonplace in many public-sector organisations. They face the same imperatives as those in the private sector. The turnaround strategy still works but the additional question of managing political stakeholders is paramount in this sector. The introduction of new management practices can also be challenging in such cultures – public sector or not. The other point this case study brings out is the burden on leadership. The CEO could not satisfy all of the stakeholders all the time and was particularly unpopular among unionised staff. So do not expect to win any popularity contest. It can also be exhausting work: beware executive burnout.

Strategies for change

The imperative for change in this zone is stark: survival. The environmental conditions are severely unfavourable and it's like being in a storm with the ship's helm broken. In short, it's a slowly unfolding disaster that looks difficult to avoid and options are running out fast.

There is only one sensible response: a radical turnaround. A study by academics and change specialists, Dexter Dunphy and Doug Stace, assessed a group of Australian service sector companies going through change.[4] They looked at the different approaches that created value or saved the firm. Organisations in the risk zone needed radical and authoritarian change masters. The government bail out of financial institutions during 2008 illustrates the point. They created stability. Change is inevitable: you do it yourself or the ravages of the environment will do it for you.

This environmentally inspired need for change comes often without warning. There will be those who simply have not been reading the signs and have been complacent. However, what we are talking about in this situation is sudden environmental shifts described as punctuated equilibrium.

The argument goes that large-scale changes are not frequent. Quite the opposite, they tend to come around periodically over years. They are driven by disruptive technology or break-through process innovations and have a profound impact on the structure of industry. The window of managing these tectonic shifts is estimated at a couple of years. Otherwise your company could fail to survive or will remain at a competitive disadvantage.

Radical turnaround is not easy but it is clear. The characteristics of this approach are well known. Typically, the pace of change is fast and intense. Restructuring takes place, often associated with layoffs. The intention is that the impact and scope of the changes are system-wide rather than incremental, which would never do the job. It marks a severe reorientation and 'the way we did things in the past' will come to an end.

[4] Dunphy, D., and Stace, D. (1993) 'The Strategic Management of Corporate Change', *Human Relations*, 46, 8, pp.905–20.

Navigating through this type of strategic change

This type of strategic change is fast-paced, radical and direct. How can organisations successfully navigate through it? Let's look at the practical applications by examining a division of Lloyds TSB, a UK bank.

In 2004, it seemed as if Lloyds TSB Retail Banking had lost its way. Confidence was low. Income and profits were below competitors and performance was below the high street benchmark – for example, the cost income ratio was almost 50 per cent more than the market leader. Morale was low and the deputy CEO, Mike Farey, had the uneasy task of holding the reins while awaiting the arrival of a new boss.

He did not have to wait long. Terri Dial, ex-CEO of Wells Fargo, arrived in June 2005. Dubbed as the 'human cyclone' for her passionate management style in the United States, she is credited for the changes at Wells Fargo that made it one of the most successful US banks. She wasted no time reviewing the Lloyds TSB landscape.

Lloyds TSB had been the biggest bank in the world and, under Sir Brian Pitman, had seemed unassailable. By the time Dial joined the board, Lloyds TSB was suffering from indigestion caused by the £7.3 billion acquisition of Scottish Widows in 2000, and its confidence had been dented when it failed to buy Abbey National in 2001. Customer satisfaction was plummeting and the bank's market share falling.[5] Terri Dial quickly concluded that the bank needed to do something different.

It wanted clear blue water from its rivals. The answer was simple. Change, she made clear, was inevitable and unless Lloyds TSB kept up with its customers' habits and lifestyles, it would eventually become obsolete.[6] She wanted to make a difference and understood the clock was ticking.

[5] *Sunday Times* (2006) 'Human cyclone hits Lloyds TSB, will Terri Dial be able to change things fast enough to satisfy her City critics?', 17 December.

[6] Ebrahimi, H, (2006) 'The Interview: Lloyds' UK boss Terri Dial'. *Financial Mail*, 27 November.

The clarion call from the executive team and Eric Daniels, the CEO, was to 'Become Britain's most recommended bank'. So that was the task. The retail network had 1,850 branches across the United Kingdom, accounted for over 40 per cent of pre-tax profits and had 21 per cent market share in the retail sector. The feedback from Dial's initial visits to branches and talking with customers was resounding: it was time to put the customer first.

Dial was no stranger to change. At Wells Fargo she added considerable value by introducing the concept of the branch as a store in much the same way Wal-Mart would think of its branches. Thus, customer experience was the key to gaining ground. She found that people were generally happy with the core services of transactions but the failure to create a relationship meant lost sales opportunities. Thus, the birth of the 'stores concept' was introduced to Lloyds TSB. It started with a series of workshops, DVDs, in-house TV and discussions with senior managers to socialise the concept and create a sense of purpose. This was the beginning of the 1,000-day plan to revolutionise the bank's retail operations.

The second phase was to match talk with action. A major and swift restructuring took place. The entire network was slimmed down to four mega stores, 18 regional areas and then the branch network. It meant the closure of 19 branches and taking some criticisms from local communities. Dial commented:

> 'A retail network has to move and adapt to the way that the community moves. A 10-year promise just does not make sense any more. Ten years is a lifetime. And a branch network is alive. So we have to make sure that we are where the people are.'

Thus, the movement of ideas, strategic initiatives and feedback up to the top reached new heights.

The intent was to gain more returns from the network and focus on reorientation and alignment of each store outlet. Ron Whatford, the internal change guru, was tasked with this role. His first question was: What is the purpose of the store? 'I wanted to know why we were doing this and what was the expected outcome? At first people did not know what I was talking about. But eventually, they got it and that helped us get their early engagement and ideas into the process.'

The purpose of the store was to realise the bank's strategic ambitions, be a channel to market and be the place to meet customer needs. The focus on customers meant that the bank took the decision to cut back office costs and redeploy the resources on customer services, training tiller clerks with selling skills, targeting clients as they came through the door for types of services and providing more support to stores through a Stores Warehouse. The initiatives drew upon Six Sigma methodology, an approach that drives for efficiencies and lean manufacturing.

Lloyds TSB piloted the new concept stores in 30 places: for example, at the Oxford Street branch in the West End of London and Cheapside in the City. Refurbishments played an important part during this phase.

Gaining significant efficiencies and realignment created a buzz and excitement in the place. I recall being in Ron Whatford's office on 27 November 2007. It was the day the UK electronic banking system went down and you could feel the sheer delight that Lloyds was the only bank to be able to get up and running within 24 hours. The level of responsiveness in the back office and the systems supporting the front-line stores simply amazed me.

These changes created better cycle times to process transactions and gained productivity. However, that was only half the plan. The real challenge was changing the customer experience. A new wave of initiatives followed and making customers feel valued and operating effectively become the two drum beats of the bank.

The next steps used factual data to drive change and behaviours. Consider this scenario. You enter your bank at three o'clock in the afternoon just before picking up the children and it's full. There are four counters but only two clerks at the desk and others seem to be wandering in the back office chatting and generally unconcerned by the increasing numbers in the queue. You walk away hacked off. You never want to use the bank's services again and you become a 'detractor': someone who recounts the awful experience at the next party. Social network theory suggests that such a story will pass quickly to like-minded people. The ones you do not want to alienate. So bad news travels fast. It impacts sales and profits.

This is exactly the sort of problem Ron Whatford's team aims to prevent. They have introduced a new scheme of actively reviewing the customer experience. After each day of visits a random number of customers is called to get a rating of the experience the previous day. Ratings of 0–4 mean a detractor, 5–7 are the middle ground and 8–10 are 'promoters' who would recommend the bank to their friends, family and associates.

Three things follow:

1 More information is gathered to understand why the customer would recommend and promote so that the bank can do more.

2 The store manager or the customer service manager also calls the customer to hear the feedback directly.

3 Each store is given a score based on the net sum of promoters or detractors. Those with low net scores get a message and an invitation from Terri Dial to tell her what the manager is going to do to improve the scores.

Hundreds of emails are exchanged. Some managers say they will manage the queue better. Feedback to one clerk suggested that all that was required was a smile. Another clerk moved the plant pot so that parents could get their buggies in and out more easily. There were thousands of little things but they all made a huge impact.

Did it make a difference? You bet. Revenues increased to £1,808 million. Cost income ratios improved compared to the competition and the selling cycle time was halved. Terri Dial moved in April 2008 to join Citigroup to spread her magic dust there as well. Lloyds TSB later moved on to acquire HBOS.

Common themes

The Lloyds TSB case brings out some common themes – clarity of goal, change follows strategy and the role of leadership. However, three receive additional attention:

1 The focus of change was putting the customer first. This began with recognising how customer retention drove revenues at the strategic level. It then followed through with customer feedback after customers left the 'store' through to little but meaningful changes such as moving the plant pot. There's a clear line of sight between vision and execution.

2 There are multiple levels to the process. The big strategic planks precede restructuring, which in turn provides the opportunities for pilot projects and then implementation of regular system checks to maintain momentum.

3 Pilot projects are a great way to test ideas, gather data and get traction and buy-in as well as quick wins.

Implementing this sort of change

So how can managers implement this sort of change? It is not easy and this was the challenge that is illustrated in the next example.

Trying to overcome inertia

Peter Volter (not his real name) was director of engineering for a UK, transport and network system. His approach to life was generally direct and his attention to detail without fault. He could easily work his way through a deck of 90 slides of graphs and numbers and tell you the key performances and trends of all the main activities within his business. If it could be measured, then it could be controlled and managed. This dictum formed a part of his managerial style. He was tough but fair.

Thus, Peter seemed to be the ideal candidate for CEP, the integrated train network company that hired him. The company's performance record was poor compared with its competitors'. It was chronically late, drawing an unacceptably high number of passenger complaints. Productivity and cycle times were low. The government's audit agency saw CET as a poor performer, and passenger groups called for more resources and serious government attention. The company was given a couple of years to turn the situation around – or face takeover by another network.

Peter's experience as a career engineer in a variety of international assignments meant that he knew exactly what to do: make sure stock is in the right place; set tight schedules on maintenance and safety; improve staff performance; and ensure you have the right talented people in the right place. Unfortunately, the problem was more fundamental, and he wasn't sure how to go forward. Should he start by telling his people what to do or by selling the case for change? How could he manage the time pressures and the threat of external events? How could he establish trust as the new boss and yet drive through these changes? Was he to become a hero or a villain?

His first step was to set the direction and vision of what he wanted the company to look like in a couple of years. He visited local depots, had meetings with local engineers and listened to their concerns. It started well.

In addition, he drew on industry standards to create new metrics for the senior managers and their units. He quickly set up new management processes that captured all sorts of performance data, and monthly management meetings used these reports to measure performance and evaluate progress. The packet of numbers contained everything anyone needed to know about the business. Most of the managers struggled to keep up with these new measures, much less find them useful. They simply were not used to them. 'I do not always understand the different measures,' said one in an interview.

The introduction of new work practices helped, but the speed of adoption was still relatively slow. Finally, Peter's energy and drive led him to run spot checks of the depots to see whether they had adhered to the new practices. He rolled up his sleeves to get things done, working long and late hours.

We met Peter about a year into the change process. All the company's metrics had improved, drawing praise from the government agency. Punctuality and reliability had improved. Peter had acquired more resources for the network, compensating for underinvestment in the past. Teamwork in the depots had vastly improved.

He was proud of their achievements. But some people still weren't 'getting it', he reflected. He was tired and frustrated with the slow pace of change and had the nagging suspicion that if he walked away tomorrow, everything would default to the old bad habits. He wasn't sure what else to try and sought another perspective.

We needed to understand why, despite the improvements, this organisation remained fundamentally inert. What were the barriers to change? What might be done next? We ran the SCi research questionnaire[7], conducted a number of interviews with senior stakeholders, and ran focus groups with employees in the depots where the vehicles were maintained, cleared and managed.

The results confirmed Peter's suspicions. What we found was an organisation that was not ready for change. Despite the exacting demands of the environment and the pressing time frames, the organisation was a change avoider and solidly in the derailment zone.

With further analysis, we found that each of the five factors scored below average or low compared to the norm group. Each of the internal capabilities lay in the danger zone. Legacy practices, traditions, the decentralised nature of the depots, union actions and a fear of the unknown led to some of the inertia. Poor communications, skill gaps and a culture of blame still existed. The internal focus of the top management team accounted for little traction for change as they didn't really understand the seriousness of the external threat.

The additional interesting point was how people experienced Peter's leadership. He was fit for purpose, a turnaround agent in a turbulent environment, pressed for time. The change process had started well, providing structure, clarity and a sense of purpose, reported most of the workers. They enjoyed Peter's enthusiasm, energy and drive. But after the first nine months or so, the more he pushed the more they went into passive retreat. Comments included: 'We do not have to do it because we know Peter will', 'He has so much energy, I don't need to worry' and 'We know now when he's coming to do a spot check. So we rush around, make busy and just do things we know he usually inspects. . . We leave stuff and rubbish around the back of the sheds. He never looks there.' We began to gain a clear picture of this undeclared dynamic between the leader and the recipients of change – the irony being that the intended drives for change created the reverse effects.

[7] The SCi questionnaire is the tool that helps diagnose your changeability. You may have already completed the questionnaire in Appendix 2 or attempted the fuller version on the website at www.ilyasjarrett.com.

We got all of the stakeholders into one room and during an afternoon session shared our data and insights. The group did the rest themselves. For the first time, people were able to share their fears, frustrations and anguish. Peter was shocked. He had not realised how his role had contributed to the journey of change. It had become overly reliant on him being the focal point.

The group decided on the next stages of the change process. They agreed to run a wider conference to get the inputs of their direct reports to share the data and get more people on board. A few months later, they did exactly that but may have already been too late. Peter became tired and frustrated, and left. Shortly afterwards, the company was taken over by another network.

Areas for reflection

The areas for reflection in this case are subtle. On the positive side, we see the use of external performance metrics as helpful, with clear goals and a sense of urgency. However, it also shows the difficulties of making change stick and staving off the inevitability of forced change in the risk zone. Yes, the company's performance improved significantly, but you might argue that it made it more attractive to sell off. The new owners have continued to make hard changes to get more from the company.

Second, it draws out the difficulty of getting the right balance as a leader. In a turnaround situation, you need to create a sense of urgency and accelerate the pace. Yet at the same time, too much push can lead to alienation of the very groups you want to change and they can absolve themselves of responsibility.

Who said it was easy?

The different cases of managers' experiences show the complexities of managing change. Turnaround styles are the most suited to organisations in the derailment zone.[8]

---

[8] Dunphy and Stace, op. cit.

The cost of turnaround is high risk. Leaders may see it as an all or nothing gamble as there is nothing to lose. But the potential for personal burnout, low traction or external events taking over remain high. Like many things in life, direction needs to be tempered with judgement, and it's important to know when to push and when to ease off.

The implication is that managers continue to have a choice. They need not be swept along by the waves of the external environment:

- The outcome and goals for change are clear: survival and reorientation. Thus, the prize for success is great and can be a huge motivator.

- Timing and pace are short and fast.

- Turnarounds share common building blocks in the process of change. Set a clear strategic direction; employ rapid restructuring; develop pilot projects to gain quick results; institute performance management; instigate a follow-up process with lots of process improvements. With so much happening so quickly, it is no wonder that change can appear as constant. It is easy to lose a sense of coherence in the seeming chaos of a change strategy.

- Managers must exercise judgement on the degree of push versus pull in driving change. They have to demonstrate commitment and inspiration but not let people off the hook or alienate them. A tough call.

- Its approach certainly creates a sense of energy and a burning platform.

The difficulties are apparent:

- The risk of failure is high – for the organisation, the people involved and those leading it.

- Environmental conditions may outpace the ability to change. Inertia can stymie change even in the face of destruction, and companies can face catastrophic consequences – look no further than Pan Am and Lehman Brothers.

- The loss of the organisation's purpose, meaning and soul can be traumatic for the people who remain and they are left with a sense of guilt and anger from the process.

▌ The personal and emotional toil on managers can also be a heavy burden and even personal (e.g. burnout).

▌ Mismatch of timing and the pace of change can lead to change weariness.

The challenge for managers under these conditions is that change is going to happen anyway. Their contribution is how to influence, steer and shape it so that the outcome is good for the company, its clients and stakeholders, as well as for the remaining employees. How can they manage these difficult tradeoffs?

▌ The focus for change needs a leadership group that has insights and can interpret the urgency of the situation and can respond. The chairman of the InterContinental Group appointed Andrew Cosslett when the strategy changed to divesting assets and moving out of the property market. It was not that his predecessor was doing a bad job, it was just that conditions had changed. Thus, the incumbent's leadership group may not always be best placed to drive the new changes. Helping the group to understand and gain support is the first item on the agenda. The sense of urgency remains paramount.

▌ Cut through the dominant logic of the organisation's previous implicit and unchallenged practices. The best way to sever these is to set up task-based, goal-orientated groups that work across functions and usual work groups. They are given clear output goals that are managed as programmes and projects over explicit deadlines. These groups are directly accountable to the senior leadership group. The value of this approach is that it attacks any dysfunctional organisational dynamics as well as breaking down old structures. It also delivers visible outputs.

▌ Changing the culture under pressure is like making a curry with a hot flame and insufficient time for the powder and spices to infuse the food. It means you can still taste the powder in the final meal. It's the same with changing culture. In the longer term, engagement strategies that take the people with you are also important to repair the trauma of change and maintain sustainability.

▌ Rebuilding organisational capabilities is important once the cruel weather abates. It will also be the time to look at those scanning capabilities. Is there anything else that could have helped us predict changes that caught us out in the first place?

Zone	Adaptive strategies for change	Characteristics of strategy	Risks or negative outcomes
Derailment	'Reforming' or turnaround – ripping up the old and dictating the new	Punctuated change: rapid, focused and 'aggressive'	It is only a temporary excursion, default to old ways and potential for failure and demise; high risks

Summary

▌ Organisations in the risk zone are vastly out of alignment with their environment and can derail.

▌ Companies have choices but how these play out are a complex interplay among leadership, internal capabilities and the external environment.

▌ Radical turnaround strategies tend to be the most successful but require a clear strategic direction, structure, pace and timing in order to work.

▌ Managers matter and their leadership styles can make a difference between success or failure.

Beware the 'comfort zone'

He who lets the sea lull him into a sense of security is in very grave danger.

Hammond Innes

T he music business can be unforgiving. You can find yourself at the top of the charts overnight and fall from grace with even greater speed. The economics mean that only one artist in a thousand makes it to the top. Even fewer manage to stay there.

Consider Sam, a British artist who produced vibrant and original music and began to develop an increasingly higher profile on the London music scene, supporting well-known bands. It was an exciting time in the young musician's career. However, the additional attention and recognition meant that Sam became overconfident and a little complacent; at least for a while, he was seduced by his new life and took his eye off the important things. Before long, playing second fiddle behind the big names became a habit. He delayed his new ideas to enjoy the limelight and began to live beyond his means. If you ask about Sam now, people in the business say, 'Yeah, I remember him. He had great promise.'

Complacency sets in

The same is true for organisations. They make a name for themselves; they are successful and able to operate in times of change. And then complacency sets in. They lose their way and forget to keep trim. In their 1982 book *In Search of Excellence*, consultants Tom Peters and Bob Waterman profiled successful companies and tried to isolate the reasons for their good fortune. The authors held up the companies – including the likes of Wang, Xerox and IBM – as examples of how a strong culture creates a source of advantage. The companies were praised as paragons of change. And then, within a few years of the book's publication, many of the companies found themselves locked into their own dominant logic, complacent and seduced by the comfort zone. These corporate superstars were forced to reinvent themselves in order to survive.

What is the comfort zone?

The comfort zone – zone three – is similar to the steady state zone in that the external environment tends to be placid or at least changes are slow or predictable. The difference is that unlike the companies in zone one, these in zone three do have the ability change. The problem is that they do not take advantage of their spare change capabilities. Instead, companies get familiar with the environment, lack urgency and gain a false sense of invulnerability. The zone represents a misalignment between the demands of the external world and the organisation's strategic change capability. Here we have a situation of 'organisational slack'.[1]

Performance outcomes tend to be satisfactory, and thus the drive for change or improvements can be low. Contrary to this state, the extra 'time' could be used to generate new strategies, create products or process innovations, or exploit untapped market opportunities. It could thus provide an opportunity to use underdeployed resources to greater efficiency, R&D or more exploration strategies.

How does a company know it is in the comfort zone?

Transport Co. certainly knew. It could have coasted along for some time. However, it decided to break the spell and explore instead.

[1] The term was coined by Cyert, R.M. and March, H.A. (1958) *A Behavioural Theory of the Firm*, Prentice Hall, New Jersey.

Transport Co.

Transport Co. operated as a sheltered monopoly, having been newly privatised in Far Eastern Asia. The environment experienced low levels of competition and was not constrained by resources. The company was internationally renowned for its culture of innovation and technological advancement.

Its leadership group was seen by the SCi research survey as insightful. In scanning, the group used international benchmarks as competition and took pride in developing new ideas for the industry and maintaining its international reputation. (See Chapter 3 for a reminder of these ideas.)

The company had a culture of adaptiveness characterised by innovation and learning and inspired by visionary leadership. Employees displayed openness and an appetite for strategic change, always looking for opportunities to improve their transport vehicles and processes. These features were matched by matrix and project-based processes. Feedback showed that most of middle management agreed that Transport Co. had a highly flexible approach and that the system provided a loosely coupled structure. It facilitated fast implementation of ideas, information and feedback loops, so that everyone felt involved.

Naturally, some political difficulties persisted and some people resisted change. We know from Chapter 6 that such a response is natural. Disagreements didn't just disappear. But in the spirit of *kaizen*, the philosophy and practice of continuous improvement and fluid execution, conflicts and differences were managed with respect and openness.

Transport Co. saw a progressive growth in both operating profit and return on assets over a five-year period. The danger of being comfortable and overconfident with its privileged position was an issue that troubled both the shareholders and the leadership. The risk was that it could become complacent. However, the discussions on this risk and relative openness among the top management team ensured that the issue of change was regularly reviewed at the board level. The diverse members of the board had a fresh perspective and guarded against the lapses of omission.

The group adopted a 'deforming' strategy for change. It would have been all too easy to stay in the comfort zone; instead, the company set out to actively challenge itself. Transport Co. demonstrated an appetite for product and service innovation by introducing complementary business models to feed revenues into its core operating services of transport. These have been based on building business and institutional communities around its main transport network hubs. In addition, it has started investments and new operations in adjacent geographic markets and is looking to grow internationally with asset-light models and joint ventures with local international partners.

Here is a company that could become complacent by sticking to its core business and domestic market but has used its organisational slack for innovation and reframing the traditional models of transport companies.

The adoption of 'deforming' strategies of challenging successful dominant logic means that mindsets need to change and that adaptation through engagement is necessary.

Lessons learned

Transport Co. lay in the comfort zone. Its near monopoly position made it easy for it to do nothing more than the minimum. Keep market dominance and use its advantage inappropriately. Instead, we see three sources of influence that stop complacency:

1 The external board and shareholders are agitating for more. It is not enough to see 'satisficing' behaviours or results; they want the company to optimise its opportunities. In many ways, these stakeholder groups represent the pressures from the external world. This draws out the importance of good governance, transparency and the responsibility held by non-executive and shareholder groups.

2 The executive leadership group also shares the drive to operate against the tide. They score high on scanning as well as reading and interpreting opportunities. Their insightfulness favours shaking the place up so as to move into new markets along with striving for excellence.

3 Their internal organisational capabilities foster collaboration and an attraction to innovation – in products and process.

The imperative for change in this zone is not always clear. Most will see it as an opportunity to enjoy the benefits of an easier time and fail to understand the dangers that lurk below the water's surface. When Motorola was at the top of its game and the then CEO Bob Galvin announced that there were difficult times ahead, most of his fellow directors and staff thought he was mad. Two years later, his worries became reality, but it was too late: Nokia had arrived.

This is a period when the organisation is far from stretched, and the concern is that chronic complacency will set in for ever. The change imperative is neither immediate nor threatening. It tends to take a visionary leader to comprehend both the advantages and the pitfalls of this unique situation.

The main change strategy during times of organisational slack is to make hay while the sun shines. The options are considerable, and this strategy requires 'insightful' leadership in order to be most effective.

We never had it so good

'Most of our people have never had it so good.' The then British prime minister Harold Macmillan coined this phrase to assign credit for the rising economy of the late 1950s to the Conservatives. The slogan could equally be applied to the pharmaceutical industry in the 1990s.

The global pharmaceutical industry includes thousands of companies in its fold: drug manufacturers, wholesalers, research organisations and biotech firms. The top tier of about a dozen multinational firms is often dubbed 'Big Pharma' and their sales account for roughly half of the world's estimated $700 billion retail drug market. But the pharmaceutical industry is relatively fragmented, with the biggest companies, such as Pfizer, holding less than 10 per cent of the global market.

For decades, the industry appeared unstoppable. The world's population was ageing in both developed and developing economies, patents held off competition, and a steady stream of blockbuster drugs hit drugstore shelves.[2]

As an article in *The Economist* put it, 'Big Pharma firms are in a business to die for.' Global drug sales have almost doubled since 1997 and are expected to continue rising. Compared with counterparts in other industries, most big pharmaceutical companies have been hugely profitable, with operating margins over 25 per cent, against 15 per cent or so for most consumer goods.[3] For the most part, these were halcyon days, and few companies set out to revamp their business models. They became comfortable and complacent.

So how does a company break out of the comfort zone? A shift in the environment itself can be an initial spark. The past few years has seen the landscape change. Many key drug patents are due to expire, with some $70 billion worth of drugs facing a challenge by generic rivals.[4]

Signs of imminent change are already here. In 2006, the Thai government shook the industry in overruling international patents for Efavirenz, an anti-retroviral drug made by Merck, and switching to a Thai-made generic copy at half the price. Big Pharma has tried other strategies – for example, negotiating with generics manufacturers to delay their drugs coming onto the market. Novartis, a big Swiss firm, drew up a private settlement for India-based Dr Reddy's to delay the launch of a generic rival to Exelon, Novartis's Alzheimer's remedy. Some have produced their own generics. According to a survey[5] of global branded-drugs firms, a third of them launched authorised generics between 2005 and 2007 – and the number will grow to 44 per cent between 2008 and 2010. Pfizer has set up an in-house division to handle such generics. However, most of these strategies remain in the same paradigm using the same business model.

[2] *The Economist* (2002) PwC quoted in 'Poor practices, Trouble in the making', 29 August (Sloppy manufacturing comes under fire, but inefficiency is the real problem).

[3] *The Economist* (2005) 'Prescription for change', 16 June.

[4] Ibid.

[5] *The Economist* (2008) 'The bitterest pill', 24 January.

Drug-company sales have declined to single-figure growth from 10–15 per cent annual increases for most of the 1990s. Pipelines for new drugs seem to have dried up. Despite increases in R&D expenditure of 6 per cent per year since 1995 (see Figure 10.1), the number of new drugs on the market has fallen. Furthermore, poor press and the withdrawal of some high-profile drugs has tarnished the reputation and trust of the industry. The increased cost of bringing drugs through the regulation of the US Food and Drug Administration adds to the industry's burdens.

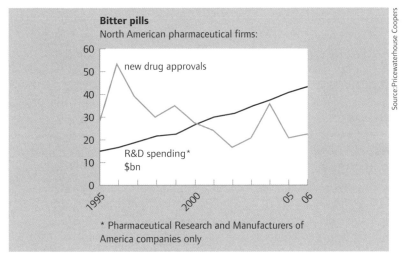

FIGURE 10.1 R&D spending against new drug approvals

The prevailing model of finding the big blockbuster, keeping the generics out by means of patents, and then marketing it to rich nations is seriously under threat.

Most companies caught a cold by acting too slowly in the face of impending change. One stands out in trying to do something different: shaking off the dominant logic of the industry and seeking to change before it is too late.

Strategies to break out of the comfort zone

Founded over a century ago, Roche has grown to become a global player, with 79,000 employees worldwide. The Swiss giant is changing and breaking the paradigm. Instead of going with the crowd, Roche is trying something different. The company targets its efforts on niche markets rather than mass markets. It is using the advantages of new technology, gene therapies and specific ailments to create new markets. Roche is moving away from the conventional logic of 'one size fits all' to creating new markets of 'personalised medicines'.

'We see a day,' wrote CEO Severin Schwan in 2007, 'when treatment choices will be based on a patient's genetic makeup, not trial and error, and when treatments will be tailored to the biology of patients' diseases, not symptoms. This is our vision of personalised medicine.'[6]

This vision helps to explain the $3 billion hostile takeover bid for Ventana Medical Systems, a US diagnostics firm. Roche has hoovered up several diagnostics and genetic-testing firms making technologies that enhance the value of its targeted cancer therapies. The firm completed a $155 million takeover of 454 Life Sciences, which makes gene-sequencing technology, and spent some $273 million on NimbleGen, which makes technologies used in identifying the genetic causes of disease.

Roche is a company that is ready to change. 'Our strategy remains firmly focused on innovating healthcare,' chairman Franz Humer wrote in January 2008. 'In the medium to long term, our global research network, strengths in biotechnology and leadership as a developer in diagnostic products will remain sources of competitive advantage in a rapidly changing healthcare market.'[7]

According to our own research, Roche displayed a high readiness across all parts of the organisation. Judging by the strategy of personalised medicines, management insights are clear to see. A decade ago, Roche had a 'me too' strategy of seeking the big blockbuster; now the company was stepping out from the crowd. How did Roche mobilise for change and avoid the drift of its competitors?

[6] Roche CEO in the 2007 Annual Report.

[7] Letter from Roche chairman in the 2007 Annual Report.

The company's strategic insights about the market and detecting the change in trends is the first difference. It is not a short-term hit – it forms part of Roche's core capability as management constantly scans the environment for new partnership opportunities and segments or niche markets. Despite changes at the top, things are staying on track.

Franz Humer moved to chairman, Severin Schwan to CEO. Schwan intends to keep focused on the company's strategic insights to concentrate on pharmaceuticals and diagnostics businesses rather than big acquisitions. He previously headed up diagnostics at Roche so knows the business. He has been described by some as 'a courage man', having a good balance of continuity and freshness. 'I don't see any change in strategy,' he says. 'You can realise some value with big acquisitions, but there is a big risk of value destruction at the same time.'[8]

Roche has so far been unique in pursuing a twin-pillar strategy, combining drugs and diagnostics tools in the belief that medicine in the future will be tailored to individuals.

Internally, the company is similarly geared up to be responsive. It has restructured but not in the same way as in a crisis. It has done so in a sustainable way to maintain long-term benefits. It needs to be both flexible and adaptive to gain value from smaller niche markets. Cumbersome processes, slow responses and poor communication would lead to certain failure. Roche has posted increases in revenues and profitability for the past few years as a result of this strategy. Its processes, structures and execution flow from the strategy. It is a company that has stepped outside the alluring zone of complacency. These moves to change continue.

In 2007, Roche's sales were $40.1 billion, up 10 per cent – the highest in the industry. It topped its Swiss arch-rival Novartis by $2.4 billion. Something seemed to be working and its share price in 2007 was high (see Figure 10.2).

[8] Reuters (2007) November at:
http://www.reuters.com/article/innovationNews/idUSWEA643720071108?pageNumber=1&virtualBrandChannel=0

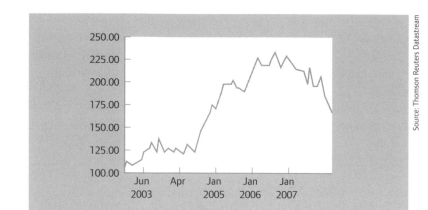

Source: Thomson Reuters Datastream

FIGURE 10.2 Roche share prices, 2003–2007

So how can managers implement this sort of change?

What might be some of the difficulties along the way and how might they be overcome? Consider Financial Products Company Europe and its attempts to implement change in this zone.

Financial Products Company Europe

The top team of Financial Products Company Europe called us in to help with the problem of 'feeling stagnant' – a difficult concept to understand. What did they really mean? We talked to each of the members of the top team using a structured interview process, along with some of the managing directors of the country offices. It didn't take long to reach a conclusion: the company was stuck in a rut. It had high levels of market penetration in most markets, good market share (in the top three in most of the major markets), and an outstanding brand. Financial Products ran efficiently and generally exhibited medium to high levels of change capability, but management never felt moved to fully tap the company's internal dynamic capability.

Our first step was to engage management in a strategic conversation. What did they want to achieve and why? A small workshop with the top team helped create an agenda for change. They wanted to see more vitality, bigger margins and something that would make them stand out from their competitors. It also revealed that while they had a good understanding of the markets, this did not translate down to the country offices in a consistent manner.

Based on further consultations and face-to-face interviews with country directors and specialists, we designed a three-day conference for the European boss, his executive team, country managers and their executive teams. The group of about 60 people represented the company's key assets.

There were **three things** that helped make a difference to Financial Products' ability to change and its financial fortunes. Each team was primed with a set of questions about its current operations, markets, clients, segments and aspirations.

The first day helped them understand, refresh or **redefine their strategic positioning** by using the data collected during the pre-work phase. Standard strategy models were used, focusing each market's attention on its most profitable action points. The next day, each team was asked **to set out a plan of execution**. They identified barriers and got peer feedback from other teams as to how to break logjams.

I vividly recall the final day. Each team proudly presented its plans, showed how it would meet its goals and basked in the glory of three days' hard work and fun. The presentations had to that point been the highlight of the conference, and we could hear the rattle of cutlery as lunch was prepared. What a great morning's work!

It was then, at 11.45 a.m., that we made the announcement. The task for each team was **to find a way to improve what it had already achieved**, to **vastly exceed planned targets** and tell us how it planned to proceed. For example, how could the team double profitability? How could penetration rates be improved? How could it increase customer repeat business by another 10 per cent? Each team was given a challenge that met its market conditions.

You can imagine the reactions. 'It's unrealistic,' said one managing director. 'We have thought of everything,' said another. 'I don't care for this game any longer,' said a third. It was like facing a group of hostile fans from the opposite team. How could the mood change so quickly? Then a voice boomed through the noise. 'We are going to do this for real. Otherwise, the three days will have been a complete waste of time. Each one of you could do this in your own office. I'm serious. We have to do something different.' It was the CEO. People drooped back to their groups.

At first, the room lacked any energy. I feared we'd spoiled a great few days. But after half an hour, the tone picked up with little murmurs and discussions within each team. An hour later, there was the hum of groups working. After another two hours, we had the beginnings of some new propositions on the table. Each idea again faced the challenge of the other teams. The robust test of each proposal made them stronger.

In reality, the new propositions differed in quality: a third were truly innovative and creative adaptations, a third added value, and the last third were examples of fine-tuning and process improvements. But I remember travelling back through the mountains of Europe, wishing I had been paid on a percentage basis for the additional value the teams created that afternoon.

What are the characteristics of this approach?

The characteristics of this type of approach are as follows:

▌ All strategies focus on the future. A look at the current situation will create too little interest and traction to warrant change.

▌ Buy-in by the top leadership is critical. Again it is different in nature from the other zones. Top leadership provides the legitimacy for thinking outside of the norm. We saw this in all three cases.

▌ Strategies are often intentionally disruptive to bring attention to the potential dangers and opportunities. Transport Co. could have easily stuck to its core products but worked tirelessly on additional services to gain extra value.

▌ It builds on intrapreneurial talent. As a result, the approach is both emergent and exploratory. Leaders of change need to show persistence, conviction and courage. Prophets in their own land are seldom welcome.

▮ It has to challenge existing mindsets and dominant assumptions. It is easy to be satisfied with the current level of performance. In the case of Financial Products Company Europe, breaking the mindset of complacency was done by challenging mental models, practices and expectations.

▮ Organisations need to be ambidextrous – so, for example, ideas that grow can be explored and exploited through a selective sub-business unit while the wider organisation continues to operate on its efficiency frontier.

▮ Outcomes may include product innovations, spin-offs, joint ventures and perhaps unusual partnerships with other organisations. For example, the low-cost airline Go Fly successfully grew out of its lumbering parent British Airways. A management buy-out was financed by 3i, the venture capitalist, and the company was eventually sold to easyJet.

▮ Strategies focus on optimising underused resources in new situations such as markets, or in products.

These strategies need to be led. They will not happen voluntarily – the comfort of this zone does not lend itself to change.

These actions are similar to taking regular exercise after the racing season is over. You still need to train to build up muscle strength and stamina. They can also be compared to docking up ship for a few weeks and going beyond the essential repairs. You are typically looking for opportunities to improve the performance of your craft and anticipating the different situations that you may face going forward.

Exploit core capabilities

Companies need to exploit their core capabilities rather than letting them wither on the vine. Situations will vary according to circumstances. However, we saw in the case of Financial Products Company Europe how that company was challenged to use the knowledge of the market to seek out better returns rather than be satisfied with average returns.

It also means that the organisational culture would have to be primed or predisposed to change. It would need to display:

▌ openness to learning

▌ a performance-management imperative

▌ an ability to build on the creativity in the organisation.

The implication of this response is that managers can transcend the inertia of success and be aware of its dangers. They need not be confined to swamps of inertia.

The pros and cons

The advantages are that:

▌ It reorients and sets the strategic compass for the organisation.

▌ It helps gain early traction for change and challenges complacency.

▌ It uses underemployed resources.

▌ It seeks to engage multiple stakeholders.

▌ It seeks to release organisational creativity in the form of products, markets, new relationships and partners.

▌ It can stop the unseen rot of inertia.

The pitfalls include:

▌ Poor insight leading to doing the wrong thing.

▌ Not engaging people.

▌ Being so far out that nobody knows what you are talking about.

▌ Some risk and dips in performance in doing things differently.

▌ You abandoning ship and returning to the default routine before seeing through the results of the change.

What should managers do?

Types of generic change strategies would include the following under 'make hay':

- Create a disruptive vision.

- Scan for new opportunities that lie outside of your company's current markets or sphere of influence.

- Use scenario-planning methods that envision different situations; you have to work out your strategic responses based on those assumptions.

- Do not accept the status quo. Question all prevailing assumptions.

- Carry out an extensive engagement strategy to involve people in the future.

- Build up, repair and strengthen internal capabilities that lie low or that are underused.

- Look for structural stickiness: areas that have silos or poor structural relationships that create unhealthy conflicts or are vague. It is easier to change and enhance these potential problems now than when the system is under threat.

Zone	Adaptive strategies for change	Characteristics of strategy	Risks or negative outcomes
Comfort	'Deforming' – redefining or reframing through values and behaviours – sails full out	Need to create disconfirming reality and challenge current paradigms and assumptions; engage and involve key stakeholders	Complacency and lose competitive edge

Summary

- The comfort zone is seductive – it can lead to waste, inefficiencies and missed opportunities. It tends to make a virtue out of underutilising core capabilities or assets.

- Companies in this zone suffer misalignment between the external environment and their internal capabilities.

▌ We see examples of companies that buck the trend and use this zone as an opportunity to be seized rather than a risk to be managed.

▌ Consulting to such situations can also be risky: resentments can arise, as executives think they are doing well already. So why change?

▌ Beware the rocks of complacency. They harbour the potential for organisational destruction.

▌ Reframing the nature of the business landscape, its operating model and basic assumptions form a critical part of successful change.

Exploring the 'Zen zone'

The pessimist complains about the wind; the optimist expects it to change; the realist adjusts the sails.

William Arthur Ward

The Zen zone is like 'flow'. The world moves fast and so does the organisation. They are aligned; there is organisational adaptability. You will hear sportsmen and women talk about being in the zone. Well, this is it.

Pete Goss, MBE, is a British adventurer and entrepreneur. Quietly spoken, his wealth of experience glows through his warm eyes. He will tell his stories as if we were in front of a pub fire in the English countryside on a dark, winter's evening. His smile evokes mischief.

My favourite story was the dramatic rescue of a fellow competitor in the 1996 round the world race, the Vendée Globe. It is a non-stop, single-handed yacht race. Pete remembers how he heard the Mayday distress call and checking his wet maps found that the Frenchman Raphael Dinelli was about 160 miles away. Even worse, the damaged yacht was facing full hurricane force conditions. It is in these moments that you have to reflect. Pete did. He thought about his boat, his family and his life. He recalls how frightening it was but it is at these junctions in life, 'You stand by your morals and principles or you don't.' It took an eternal 30 seconds to decide and with that Pete turned his boat around.

Pete showed his true and remarkable colours when it really mattered. As a result he saved the life of a now life-long friend and gained the French Légion d'honneur.

For me this story has several points. Obviously, it shows the courage of Goss in response to a call of distress. It further highlights how each challenge from the elements has to be taken in your stride. He could have easily panicked or ignored the call because of the dangers to his own life. However, it is Pete Goss's values that really strike me. It took a mere 30 seconds and he turned around. He also had the internal resources and personal capabilities as an experienced sailor to have the confidence to take the challenge head-on.

Managing change in choppy waters

Managing change in choppy waters can be similar. The clouds look threatening, competitors and sharks are out there to get you and the crew does not have the appetite for restructuring or anything else for that matter. It is especially difficult if change is not easy to undertake and does not form the dominant logic of the organisation. In such cases, it quickly falters. Some of us enjoy this sort of opportunity, like Pete, while others dread it.

Similarly, organisations that embrace and enjoy the challenges of large-scale changes will tend to have the internal dynamic capabilities to make it an engaging challenge rather than a miserable experience. They constantly scan and make insightful sense of the environment, foster internal collaboration and work through cultural barriers to achieve fluid execution. They tend to thrive from each wave. They want to learn how to do things better. They see the rewards of success – from personal development to organisational performance. People in these types of organisations do not have to be press-ganged into action. They do it of their own volition. They are also supported by the leadership and systems that make it easy to turn ideas into action.

Organisations that have the internal capability to tack and turn within an external world of rapid adaptation operate in the Zen zone. They are aligned with their external environment. Here are opportunities for growth and innovation. Studies suggest that where such 'transformational' change takes place performance is greater than with those who do not undertake such changes.[1] Risks match these rewards in that less than 1 in 3 tend to succeed in such changes and the ratio can be as low as 1 in 25.[2] Thus, during the zones of opportunity the risks are also high.

The challenge for these organisations is working with complexity. The rapid nature of the environment, their own capabilities and their interactions lead to complex outcomes that simple rules are not subtle enough to cope with.

What is life like in this zone?

Pharma Co. found itself exactly in that position in 2005. You recall from the previous chapter the industry was in a turbulent state. Pharma Co. responded by beating the odds.

CASE STUDY

Pharma Co.

This was a European subsidiary that faced a huge upheaval in the market and fierce competition from its dominant rivals. Local country producers had cut margins with generics and Pharma's market share of blockbuster drugs was under threat. It was a turbulent environment and not changing was not an option.

We had a few hundred responses to the SCi questionnaire and the results showed high scores of changeability. This was shown in Pharma's leadership team being described as a thoughtful and reflective group also supported from data collected through the SCi questionnaire. The culture was adaptive and the structure was on the boundary of loosely coupled but with a strong sense of its own identity.

[1] Whittington, R., Pettigrew, A., Peck, S., Fenton, E., and Conyon, M. (1999) 'Change and Complementarities in the New Competitive Landscape: A European Panel Study, 1992–1996', *Organization Science*, 10, 5, pp.583–600; Romanelli, E and Tushman, M.L. (1994) 'Organizational Transformation as Punctuated Equilibrium: an Empirical Test', *Academy of Management Journal*, 37, 5, pp.1141–66.

[2] Whittington *et al*, Ibid.

In order to respond to this market challenge the subsidiary developed a transforming change strategy.

A small task team was put together to respond to the challenge. It was given the full support of the managing director, who had the resources and clear authority and accountability to implement their response: a market and sales strategy.

The first stage of the plan was implemented within 100 days. It focused on restructuring. It led to radical surgery on structures, processes and reporting lines. The following stages in the plan turned on an aggressive sales (and marketing) strategy. There were conflicts and disagreements through this period of change but internal organisational groups were able to resolve the substantive ones and focus on results. The group demonstrated a willingness to engage in conflicts but also had the processes in place and the maturity to resolve them for the greater interests of the company. The pressing timescale, in truth, also helped.

Over the year that followed, Pharma Co. doubled its market share, bucked the usual declining sales trend of the product life cycle and increased financial performance. The insightful nature of the strategic leadership along with a culture of openness to change provided a much needed fillip for the organisation's ability to respond quickly and effectively to changes in a fast-moving environment.

Surf the waves

The imperative for change is to surf the waves, seeing each one as an opportunity. It means that such organisations are operating at the edge and are often market leaders or among the early innovators. Innovation is not limited to new products, services or markets but also process innovation. Google, eBay or Ryanair are examples of organisations that do it well.

Complexity theory argues that in the midst of multiple interactions and spirals there lies an implicit structure. It can be difficult to understand or identify this to begin with and authoritarian, top-down models tend not to work as the knowledge is distributed. The answer to the problem can be found by engaging multiple stakeholders in the solution and treating each part with equal value.

There are some simple lessons to be learned from the above case study. It shows the importance of a clear sense of direction. A strategy for change closely follows the organisational strategy. It is bold, purposeful and engaging. It is proactive rather than reactive as in turnaround strategies or passive strategies for those operating in steady state environments. For me it also demonstrates the following:

▍ Distributed leadership – the direction is collectively agreed but it is not driven only by a single source of authority. The team was allowed to get on and make the changes happen.

▍ The speed and actions they completed in the first 100 days without major casualty demonstrated the built-in organisational flex in the structures and culture.

▍ Conflicts seem to be worked through with the greater purpose in mind. (These lessons reinforce some of the points we made in Chapter 7 on fluid execution.)

▍ It's possible to buck the trend against all the historical odds.

So what does it look like to be firing on all cylinders in this space? Apple is a company that shares many of the characteristics of one that successfully operates in the Zen zone. It's outward-looking, fast-moving, innovative and executes well. It has been acknowledged as 'The Most Admired Company' for several years, and the 'Most Innovative Company', giving a high return to shareholders over a five-year period among the Fortune 500 group and exuding a passion for innovation. It operates at the edge, successfully having moved from being just a technology company to a lifestyle brand.[3]

According to the *Innovation Tracker* report, a research company that polls top executives on US innovative companies, Apple made top of the list because of its ability to continually 'churn out' innovation. Its ability constantly to launch products and sustain a culture that is always looking for the next new thing is admirable, and not easy. Such companies not only change their own product portfolio but have redefined the industry, as well as causing a domino effect in other industries.

[3] *Business Week*, Boston Consulting Group's list of The World's 50 Most Innovation Companies; The Research Associates (2006) *Innovation Tracker*; Morris, B. (2008) 'What Makes Apple Golden?', *Fortune Magazine*, 17 March, pp.40–4.

A deeper look at Apple allows us to see what it takes to operate in a fast-moving and changing environment. By 2008 Apple was the second-largest music retailer in the United States, right behind Wal-Mart. Sales stood at $24 billion and profits rose over a five-year period to $3.5 billion, up from $42 million. Apple's 25,000 employees all share the same enthusiasm for the company. It is how they recruit – from top to bottom. Steve Jobs, their CEO, is clear that this is a differentiator. It's the culture that makes them different and that is in their people. Apple requires a special kind of workforce. It hires people who are never satisfied. 'When I hire somebody really senior, competence is the ante. They have to be smart. But the real issue for me is: Are they going to fall in love with Apple? Because if they fall in love with Apple, everything else will take care of itself. They'll want to do what's best for Apple, not what's best for them, what's best for Steve, or anybody else.'[4]

This is a company that also scans well. It can see and detect incremental movements before they turn into huge waves. 'The waves of technology, you can see them way before they happen, and you just have to choose wisely which ones you are going to surf,' says Jobs. The caution is that if you choose unwisely, then you end up wasting a lot of time and energy. But if you choose wisely change unfolds quite slowly.

The company also has formidable insights. The senior management's greatest insight was that they did not want to get into any business where they did not own or control their own primary technology. They did not want to go down the Microsoft route of licensing. While it means they do not have the same level of market share as the computing giant, their track record of innovation over the past three decades of the Mac II, the iPod and the iPhone makes Apple feel it is worthwhile.

Steve Jobs recalls when he returned to the company in 1997. He and Jonathan Ive, head of design, came up with the idea of the original iMac, a candy-coloured computer with a cathode-ray tube that looked like some caricature of the future. They took the idea to the engineers and they came up with 38 reasons why it could not

[4] Morris, B., Ibid.

be done. Jobs was adamant. He insisted, 'It could be done,' and because of his sheer force of belief they begrudgingly did it. It became a big hit, outstripping sales beyond expectations.[5]

The question of control is key to Jobs's and Apple's success. Operating in an increasingly networked world of gadgets that talk to each other it is easy to imagine one company making the software, another the hardware and before long it's no longer working. Jobs says: 'The innovation can't happen fast enough. The integration isn't seamless enough. No one takes responsibility for the user interface. It's a mess.'[6] He's further quoted as saying: 'If you do not have control, you'll get your head handed back to you on a platter.' This insight is a guiding principle for the company. Ownership of the operating system gives Apple a great deal of control over its ability to design, change and adapt. Thus, it does not have the problem of resource dependencies.[7]

We can draw a further lesson from this story. Apple's employees constantly talk about 'deep collaboration', 'cross-pollination' or 'concurrent engineering'. The company is divided on both products and function. What Tim Cook, COO, calls very faint lines. It means that the structure of teams and the culture of the organisation foster collaboration. Thus, products do not just get passed from one team to another in some simple sequence or assembly line. Such an arrangement may be fine in organisations that have a routine process or operate in a stable environment. Instead, it operates as a network of loosely coupled units so that the structure is both organic and simultaneous.

Ive reinforces the point: 'The historical way of developing products just doesn't work when you're as ambitious as we are. When the challenges are that complex, you have to develop a product in a more collaborative, integrated way.'[8] Apple's unique way of working is creating a collaborative system. The organisation is

[5] Grossman, L. (2005) 'How Apple Does it', *Time Canada*, 24 October, 166, 17.

[6] Grossman, L., Ibid.

[7] We discussed resource dependencies in Chapter 4.

[8] Grossman, L., op. cit.

adaptable and finds that it is geared to change as it rides the crests of technological new waves.

Tony Fadell, a vice-president who played a key role in conceiving and building the first iPod, notes how the 'product' constantly changes. Originally, it was the iPod: physical, cool and innovative. But as the product has morphed, it is now iTunes Music Stores and iTunes. The new iPhone follows the same tradition. Apple will not hesitate to axe a past hit. It dropped the popular iPod, the Mini, to introduce the Nano – a better product with higher margins.

You cannot mention Apple and not talk about Steve Jobs as a leader. Since returning in 1997, he has galvanised both the senior management and employees to believe in the brand, themselves and how they can create the future. He's known for taking risks and that seeps into the culture. He's a perfectionist and is incredibly resilient.

Jobs displays many qualities of an effective change agent, but we'll discuss these more in Chapter 12.

But he's not just a 'good time' leader. Apple has also weathered the difficulties of the dot-com bubble burst and product failures. Contrary to the slash and burn strategies of others, Apple did the opposite. There were no lay-offs and Jobs recounts, 'What I told the company was that we were just going to invest our way through the downturn.' In fact, their R&D expenditure went up so that they could gain a head on their competitors when the downturn was over. That's exactly what it did. It worked. And Apple will do it again next time.

We must also remember when Jobs helped the recovery of Apple. The company was under intense competition, their operating systems were poor and nothing new was being successfully developed internally. Jobs helped in revitalising the Apple. He introduced new operating systems and talent, and advised on the integration of his own company NeXT with the Apple engineers. It started a new journey for Apple and Jobs.

New projects include Apple TV and Take 2. The first design was a flop. But that is the risk and rewards of an innovative culture and an organisation that runs its ship ready to change and surf the next wave. The result of Apple's approach is that the company is growing rapidly – four times faster than the industry. The iPod has captured 70 per cent of the market. Apple is growing. It is a company ready to change.

A way of life

I call this space the Zen zone. Not because it's a religion – far from it. It is more a way of life. In this zone, a company's dominant logic is to be dissatisfied with the present, to be seeking out a better tomorrow but also be informed by deep insights about itself and its industry as well as compassion for and collaboration with colleagues to satisfy customer needs. The other thing Zen-like about this space is that things are always as they appear. Contrary strategies like investing your way out of a downturn buck the trend: taking on risk where others fear. These strategies need an inner confidence. Companies that can adapt and thrive have these qualities.

So how can managers implement this sort of change?

Mergers and acquisitions grew rapidly during the mid-2000s, peaking in 2006. It was a great opportunity for companies within financial services seeking to grow quickly and this case shows how to operate in the Zen zone. It illustrates some of the practicalities of operating in a fast-moving environment, by considering two companies that had good change capabilities but the additional challenge of different cultures.

CASE STUDY

A merger between two

The two companies merging were Large Cap and Fast Cap (not their real names). My research had already meant that I had a wealth of data from both companies and one of them I had been working with quite extensively.

The SCi data on each was interesting. Large Cap was an analyser. Its change capability was above the industry average. It had large capital reserves, a wide range of products and global coverage. Its aspirations to be a significant, global player matched with its acquisition strategy at the time. Fast Cap, on the other hand, was a small but rapidly moving regional player. It was outstanding at change, adapting to it fast. This attitude seeped through the whole organisation and its network of branches. Ideas to increase market share and capture more of its existing customers' business ranged from mobile channels to get to customers, to introducing more sophisticated products to the market. As a premier regional player, the merger provided Fast Cap with bigger pockets than its local rivals.

How do you get two companies to leverage their relative strengths in a rapidly changing and competitive environment? This was the challenge of Chief Executive, Richard Dowes (not his real name), of Europe Middle East and Africa (EMEA).

Dowes spent his initial weeks travelling and getting a sense of what was working and what needed attention in each of his main operations. He and his executive wanted to get everyone pointing in the same direction and focused on the same metrics. They also wanted to see sharing of best practice, co-operation across the different countries and a culture that suited the current organisational and environmental demands: fast-moving, collaborative with their attention on results.

Dowes decided to hold a series of top leadership forums for all of the managing directors and senior directors, a population of 150 executives. These were held in smaller groups of about 25–30 people, each over a period of four days. The whole thing was done within a few months. The idea was to gain a common vision, get people on board, share best practice and find new ways of working that could capitalise on the two companies sources of advantage. In addition, Dowes and his executive team wanted to cut through any organisational processes that were slowing down the benefits of the merger.

I remember when we were going over the final design with Dowes in his office. 'You need to be there to kick off these forums and come again towards the end to see what's agreed,' said the HR Director. 'Oh yes,' I thought. 'That'll be a first. How many times have I sat in similar meetings and asked the MD or CEO to role-model his or her beliefs.' But Dowes's response totally floored me. He got up, went next door to his secretary's office and said, 'Clear my diary for these sessions. They are important.' At that point, I knew he was serious and felt I wanted to work for this guy.

Each session had a common format but sometimes the outcomes varied. Richard Dowes kicked them off by restating the companies' global aspirations and engaging directors in both understanding the goals and translating them into their own business. These discussions were aided by detailed competitive analysis of the major player across EMEA and an identification of potential market segments. Sessions on understanding change and tools to drive change into implementation meant that each director left with a plan for their own business.

However, the bigger prize was the group having a collective discussion with the MD and several members of the executive – at every leadership forum – to identify projects for action. These hot topics arose from Q&A sessions and highlighted potential market or segment opportunities, or barriers that needed breaking down. Potential opportunities included new customer segments that operated across different geographical markets. Peripheral projects included devising a rapid IT platform and getting new products from Large Cap to Fast Cap quicker. Finally, making sure all employees understood the reasons for change and the benefits.

The lists were huge. However, each forum left with no more than five or six priority projects that were going to make a difference. A project management group was set up to track all of the initiatives across EMEA and support them to realise the benefits.

Over the next two years, most of these initiatives met their targets and created healthy benefits for the newly merged company. However, that is only half the story. In a fast-moving world we saw how Richard Dowes quickly got round to the key players to gain a sense of what was happening in the business. Good quality and detailed external competitor and market analysis sat next to information about internal best practice. So the company maintained their scanning and collective insights.

Each director took back ideas to implement actions into their markets. The real benefits were on working across organisational boundaries through projects that generated revenue opportunities and new segments, or through back office teams that cut through additional cost or unnecessary bureaucracy.

The additional value of the forums was that they fostered collaboration. Suspicion and myths broke down and new relationships formed. These networks also lasted beyond the four days. They made it easier to do business, fostered cross-visits to each other's operations and provided an informal knowledge bank – as well as enabling you to know who you were talking to when you picked up the phone. Most of all it created trust and collaboration: essential ingredients when working in the Zen zone.

The five factors we discussed in Part 2 apply to this newly merged company and proved to be working at a very high level. The case study showed how the company responded to its environment with excitement and a sense of collaboration and challenge rather than with trepidation. The case study also shows a strong commitment and high integrity by the leader while at the same time an effective engagement strategy to involve country managers and senior directors in the changes – both market facing and internally. The use of the company's process from vision and goals, engagement, prioritisation then projects to execution is one worth noting.

Lessons learned

So what are the other general lessons we can take about operating successfully in this zone?

Characteristics of this type of change strategy differ in many ways from the other zones:

▌ Companies that want to stay ahead of the foul weather and stay prepared scan, scan and scan. It's that vital radar that detects a sudden wind.

▌ The vision and strategy is central. It provides a clear rationale as to why we are doing things and the higher purpose. So people do not see themselves as putting one brick on top of another, nor as masons. They can see the whole building and its purpose.

▌ The role of leadership is to set the direction, provide a role model, empower others and create the conditions through the dynamic capabilities for change. The role is different from leading in other situations (see the next chapter).

▌ Emergent strategies will also form part of the action. The idea of mission control means that groups of people can combine their talents to implement ideas locally and how they do it is not set by management.

▌ There is a different underlying assumption about power relationships and the dominant logic of the organisation. It seeks to include a multiple range of experiences, stakeholders and knowledge to get things done rather than believing all the answers lie at the top.

▌ It also means that the culture places merit on high-level values, the higher purpose of the organisation and personal accountability. This is in conjunction with collegiate models of working. Task conflict is seen as a healthy method to get more out of each person and thus exploration is an important process. A high value is placed on ideas that make work easier, customers more satisfied or provide opportunities to gain more from existing methods.

▌ Temporary structures, ambidextrous or loosely coupled structures form the bedrock to organisational agility. This means it is easy to reallocate the crew quickly when unexpected waves occur and not founder due to a slow response. Project structures, task groups and temporary, cross-functional teams typify organisations that successfully operate in rapidly changing environments.

Avoiding the whirlpools

There are some whirlpools that also make this zone dangerous. Managers should be aware that:

▌ The risks are higher and thus failure can be just around the corner. (The best of the companies see it as learning rather than failure.)

▌ Companies can get addicted to change. They become change junkies. The higher reason is lost and the change becomes the adrenaline drive.

▌ Companies, and especially leaders, can underestimate the nature of the task as they become blasé to the challenges of change.

Managers can reap the benefits of surfing the waves of rapid external change. What more can they do?

The main danger that they face is that the organisation 'tunes out' and simply sees each wave as yet another change. And that may not always be the case. So:

▌ Keep the insightfulness and sense making among the top team alive and regularly challenged. Strategic off-sites and workshops, exposure to faculty and visiting companies outside of their industry can all be employed. Anything in fact that constantly challenges dominant organisational assumptions.

▌ Straddle chaos and order. Too much complexity leads to chaos and meltdown, not enough stifles initiative. The role of the manager is to hold the tension and trade-off between the two.

▌ Maintain the contradiction. Simplify and innovate at the same time. GE's success in acquisitions is that it developed a framework, had an integration specialist work on the deal from conception to delivery and supported the integration for a couple of years after. GE simplified the process so it created consistency, clarity and delivered the results. However, it meant that more creative time could be spent on the things that mattered: the next deal or some product innovation.

Zone	Adaptive strategies for change	Characteristics of strategy	Risks or negative outcomes
Zen	'Transforming' – moving from an oil tanker to a fleet of sailing dinghies!	Strategically orientated change that impacts on culture and structure	Change junkie sees activity as more important than insightful change

Summary

▌ Organisations that are ready to change and operate in rapidly adapting environments are aligned and are able to take competitive advantage in their situation.

▌ The benefits as well as the risks are great but the dominant logic and internal capabilities of the company allow a wider set of responses to the challenges presented.

▌ Leadership's role is to set the agenda and create the environment as high levels of stakeholder engagement are required to make this strategy work well.

▌ Managing the tensions of chaos and order, simplification and innovation, and action versus thought are the greatest challenges.

▌ Tuning out is the greatest danger.

▌ Those companies that operate effectively in this zone find it easier when new challenges come rolling down to hit the bows. It's an opportunity rather than a threat.

Leading change is a fact of life so let's do it right!

I started with the notion that:

> External Environment + Internal Capabilities + Leadership = Changeability

Leadership is the final component. It acts as the integrating force for change. To be an effective advocate of change you must also be an effective leader.

Personal mastery

12

It has been said that man is a rational animal. All my life I have been searching for evidence which could support this.

Bertrand Russell

Insanity describes someone who does the same thing again and again, but is surprised when they do not achieve a different outcome. Let me explain. What was your last New Year's resolution? Did you make it stick? For most of us the answer to the first question involves a genuine aspiration to change our lives for the better. Yet, the answer to the second question is often a disappointing acknowledgement of failure to make that change happen.

At the beginning of each year, for example, the ritual is to give up smoking, to begin eating that healthy diet, to get fit or to spend more time with the family. The fact is that within three weeks most resolutions fall by the wayside. The muesli is replaced by something laden with sugar or cholesterol, the jogging by sport on TV, tucking the children up in bed by tomorrow's all-important presentation. Resolutions fail because of a lack of individual will or stamina. Sometimes the timing is just wrong. The excuses are as many and varied as they are familiar: 'I missed a class and it was difficult to return', 'I had to work late', 'The kids were off school ill'. You have probably heard these before. You may have even used them yourself.

And yet, undeterred by our weakness and failure, we do the same things for a variety of reasons time and time again – and still nothing happens. Perhaps the most amazing thing is that we still profess surprise at our failure to drink less or cut out tobacco.

Yet, there is a group that is able to change. These diehards do something different: their commitments become reality. So what is it that they do differently? (Apart from look smug.) In my experience the people who make change stick in their personal lives do several things differently: they tend to set realistic goals; do a little every day; are motivated personally; and set up the external structures to make it easy. So, for example, they make a decision to leave work early on Wednesdays. They make sure childcare is in place. They walk to the train station for 20 minutes rather than drive. They think and manage the internal things they have control over and shape the external dimensions that they can influence. They do something different and reap the rewards of a different outcome. They are able to draw upon their own personal mastery of insight, reflection, and on-going learning. Another way to think about this is that they apply leadership to their own resolutions. (Smugness is a by-product of success!)

Managing change means managing self

We have spent most of the book illustrating how effective organisations possess dynamic routines and internal capabilities for success. The same is true for effective leaders of change: they also manage themselves. To do so requires that leaders of change have the personal insights which enable them to manage themselves.

Leaders of change draw on three levels of mastery during periods of change. They use their head, their heart and their hands.

Managing personal change

Chris's personal commitment was not a problem. But, he knew what he had to do. Feedback from his 360-degree report and personal development plan made it clear that he lacked a work–life balance. His time together with his family lacked engagement. He admits: 'I was there in body, but my mind and spirit were somewhere else. I was simply tired.' I know many managers that struggle with the same problem. 'What can I do?' they ask.

The first step for Chris was to make a commitment to spend more time at home. It started by arriving home 45 minutes earlier one evening a week. He also undertook to work at home once a month and go swimming with the kids every weekend.

At the office, he also started to set clearer priorities with each of his major stakeholders to stop behaving like a headless chicken. He focused on the important things that made a difference, where the benefits exceeded the cost and pain of each of the activities. People objected at first. They didn't like the 'new' Chris. But he continued to try to become clearer about how he could and should use his time.

Finally, Chris used his travel time to and from work more effectively. An hour's train journey each way meant he could extend his day but found it difficult to switch off once he arrived home. So he used the morning commute to get through outstanding emails or papers for the day's meetings and the evening journey was reserved for down time. So he read the paper, listened to his iPod or simply decompressed before arriving home.

Effectively and decisively, Chris decided to cut through the mindlessness that was tipping him into burnout.

The initial effects were slow. There was no big bang. Colleagues tried to pressure him to act as he did before. But, with the support of a coach and his partner, he maintained his resolve. The months went by and colleagues began to notice a difference. The outcome was improved effectiveness at work, better feedback from his stakeholders, a greatly enhanced work–life balance and a happier family. Chris worked through this change over a period of seven months, managing both the internal and external dynamics of his situation, the ins and the outs. It increased his energy levels and improved his moods, as well as providing good quality time with his young family.

Chris's story shows how hard personal change can be even when there is a lot of commitment. Change is possible with practice. But, current habits and those from our past carry forward into adulthood and can operate unconsciously. Routines and practices that gave us success can become the very thing that holds us back. This is most obviously and powerfully the case for those who lead change. Change leaders need to be as fit as their change-ready organisations in order for them to be effective and equally successful.

What makes effective change leaders?

So what makes the difference? What is the head, heart and hands of effective leadership? Teaching executives from a variety of programmes at London Business School, I often give them a short exercise to agree and rank the top characteristics of an effective change agent, someone able to make the transition from one state (usually unfavourable) to a more desired one. I ask them to draw lessons from case studies as well as their personal experiences of change. I have done this exercise 50 times or more over the past few years, covering approximately 1,500 managers.

The list is very consistent. When asked the question: 'What are the characteristics of an effective change agent?' executives from leading companies usually come up with the same ones. What do you think they were? Jot them down before looking at the list below.

The top characteristics of an effective change leader:

▌ Communication of a vision – up, down and sideways. (We obviously assume that they have one!)

▌ Energy and passion

▌ Inspirational and motivational so are able to resonate with the people around them

▌ High on integrity, honesty and transparency appropriate to context

▌ Courage to start and keep going during the tough calls

▌ Resilience and open-mindedness

▌ Emotionally intelligent

▌ Manage all stakeholders and good at networking

▌ Politically astute

- Listening
- Create a sense of urgency

So here is the question for you. On a score of 1 being the lowest to 10 being the highest, how well do you rate on each of these criteria? Which two or three areas would you like to improve in yourself? What do you need to do to increase your effectiveness?

A leader of change

Allan Leighton made his name as an advocate of change who embodies many of the qualities shown in the list above. Now as the chairman of the Post Office in the United Kingdom and as the ex-CEO of Asda, part of Wal-Mart, he continues to show his mettle as a leader of change.

Leighton has an unorthodox and direct style. I recall meeting him at Asda House in Leeds. He worked in an open-plan office, casually dressed in a T-shirt, a baseball cap and jeans. He was energetic and thoughtful. But he also had an informal approach that was popular with employees. During the major changes at Asda, he did a fantastic job communicating the vision and the strategy for change very clearly to general store managers through a variety of workshops and personal messages. He role-modelled the changes he wanted to see. He played football with the staff during the most difficult periods. Yet, at the same time, he had a tight focus on restructuring, driving down costs and implementing pilot stores for change. He was no pushover.

Leighton worked as part of a tight inner team that helped the changes become more widely owned. Archie Norman was around first as CEO at Asda but then moved to chairman, leaving Leighton in charge. But with the additional help of Phil Cox, the finance director, and Tony Campbell, who led the renewal programme, they formed the crux of change.

At the Post Office, Leighton is no different. He has been courageous in challenging old work practices while at the same time averting mass strikes. The loss of 45,000 jobs and 1,200 post offices does nothing to dampen his resolve. His informal and direct style continues. For example, he will still stop the car, get out and talk directly to a postman or woman about what it's like to work for the company. He will tell you that this is something he learned in the early part of his career while at Mars, where senior management would turn up unexpectedly and inspect things for themselves, instead of receiving distorted messages through layers of management.

'You have a relationship at the top and you have a relationship where the work takes place and you sort of miss out the bit in between,' he says. 'All the business in between is the permafrost and the business prevention squads and all that sort of stuff and once upon a time I had to be part of that and now, to a degree, I don't. I'm always getting into trouble because I go direct to people and people come direct to me.'[1]

Leighton continues his quest. He is enthusiastic as well as a realist. He is hungry for change.

What I have learned from people like Allan Leighton and the executives I have encountered in the classroom is that the dynamics for successful leadership during periods of change mirror those of the organisation. First, you must understand and be sensitive to your organisational context. Then you use critical judgement, emotional intelligence and energy to get things done. Earlier I referred to these as the head, heart and hands, and if you review the list from our executives, you can see how each of the points neatly fall under one of these labels.

Common sense confirmed

You do not have to be Allan Leighton to make a difference. Intuitively, you know what makes a difference. The list of change leader characteristics gathered from the executives is reinforced by accumulated academic research. A sample of studies gives credence and relevance to what some leaders already suspect. For example, Professor Jay Conger, a colleague at London Business School, spells

[1] Teather, D. (2007) Interview with Allan Leighton 'Singular skill of a man who relished going plural', *Guardian*, 1 June.

out the importance of vision in order to get people aligned. *Vision* on its own is a start. It also has to be communicated and shared in a way that inspires and resonates with others. Daniel Goldman, Richard Boyatzis and Annie McKee, experts in the field of emotional intelligence and leadership, draw upon a wide range of studies and examples to illustrate the importance of how *emotional intelligence* and *positive attitudes* create happier teams, less conflict and better results during change.[2] Emotional intelligence means we will be more aware about ourselves and others, we are more likely to be *good listeners* and more *resilient* during the tough times of change. Leaders who manage their social and political networks are more likely to be successful in navigating change and their careers through the organisational labyrinth.

Finally, such change agents do well on *execution*. Shona Brown, a McKinsey consultant, and Kathleen Eisenhardt, Professor of Strategy and Organization at Stanford University, demonstrate from their study of successful high-tech companies in a fast-changing world that *focus, communication* and *pilot project implementation* make a difference to change outcomes.[3] My own research and consulting experience reinforces these findings. As John Maynard Keynes, the famous economist, once said: 'Theory illuminates the obvious.'

Are you personally ready?

Sounds easy enough, doesn't it? But it is much harder to put into practice. If it weren't then there would be no broken New Year's resolutions. The fact is that managing change at a personal level requires insight – and a great deal of hard work. The world is a complex place. The reality is that events happen outside of your control. Change can come as a surprise. It can hurt. It can stop you in your tracks.

[2] Goldman, D., Boyatzis, R. and McKee, A. (2002) *Primal Leadership*, Harvard Business School Press, Boston, MA. See also, Mayer, J.D., Salovey, P. and Caruso, D.R. (2008) 'Emotional Intelligence: New Ability or Eclectric Traits?', *American Psychologist*, 63:6, pp.503–17.

[3] Brown, S. and Eisenhardt, K.M. (1997) 'The Art of Continuous Change: Linking Complexity Theory and Time-paced Evolution in Relentlessly Shifting Organizations', *Administrative Science Quarterly*, 42, pp.1–34.

The difficulties arise from our expectations and attachment to certain outcomes. When things do not pan out as we expect, or we receive a setback, we can become despondent and frustrated. Each of us has a personal predisposition to handle disappointment and stress in our own way. It is a function of personality, social and cultural background, and the socialising influence of parents, among other social contexts.

When Chris heard about further restructuring in the private client side of the business he was excited about the possibilities and started planning immediately. However, Robert, a fellow member of the executive team responded with: 'Oh no. Not another change.' He could only see gloom. What is your predisposition?

You cannot control the uncertainty of the external world, nor the outcome. However, you have a choice in your inner world. You can control how you respond. This is the secret of managing personal change and leading with purpose.

The choices start at the top – in your head – especially how you think. Our world is the subject of our own making. You will remember in Chapter 5 that leadership teams that vigilantly scanned and accurately interpreted the environment had greater changeability. We also saw how managers' blinkers stopped them from seeing the whole picture. They tended to seek confirmatory data that reinforced their existing world views. The same is true for the individual leader of change.

Studies in positive psychology by Robert Emmons of the University of California and Michael McCullough of the University of Miami suggest those people that have a positive frame of mind tend to feel better about life, are more optimistic, have fewer physical symptoms, are more likely to achieve their goals and help others more.[4]

---

[4] Emmons, R. and McCullough, M. (2003) 'Count Blessings versus Burden: An Experimental Investigation into Gratitude and Subjective Well Being in Daily Life', *Journal of Personality and Social Psychology*, 84, 2, pp.377–89. See also Ben-Shahar, T. (2007) *Happier: Learn the Secrets of Daily Joy and Lasting Fulfilment*, McGraw Hill.

So, first, you can reframe the way you see the world. **Managers can make a choice**.

The second issue is the emotional attachment we hold to things we have, expect or want. We talked about attachment in Chapter 6. The idea that we develop early attachment styles that continue through adulthood affect leaders during change. What is your attachment style? Securely attached styles tend to form good relationships, are open and trusting, deal with rejection and are seen by their colleagues as resilient and cheerful. Poorly adapted styles tend to be more suspicious of others, may find it difficult to establish lasting relationships and, in extreme cases, may be withdrawn.[5] Whatever your style, creating a secure base internally or externally, so things work smoothly, is the secret of being a successful change agent.

Those who are high on emotional awareness and intelligence are more personally resilient and able to manage ambiguity. They are also more likely to understand others.

Beware the rocks of derailment

Leading change on the inside also means managing social relationships on the outside. A series of studies that started in the early 1980s by a group of American academics tried to identify what made successful executives.[6] The researchers were trying to answer the billion-dollar question. Much to their surprise, they found out instead what goes wrong and how managers can derail. This led to a rich stream of work on what became labelled 'executive derailment'.

The term 'executive derailment' was originally used to describe a person who had been very successful in their managerial career but

[5] A fuller description of attachment theory and its application can be found in Holmes, J. (1993) *John Bowlby & Attachment Theory*, Routledge, London.

[6] Mcall, Jnr, M.W., Lombardo, M. and Morrison, A.M. (1998) *The Lessons of Experience: How Successful Executives Develop on the Job*, Lexington Books, New York,. The Centre for Creative Leadership was also involved in a number of these original and subsequent studies.

who failed to live up to their full potential as the organisation saw it. How the organisation responded – fire, demote, pass over for promotion, forced resignation – spelt the end of career progression in that company. It is notable in the derailment research that the very skills that were the original sources of success are often the fatal flaws of despair. So the leader who has an outstanding track record in achieving performance targets becomes over-demanding. Another who is decisive can turn into the one who never listens and knows it all. It is another form of competency trap but at the personal level. (See Chapter 8.)

Typically, leaders who derailed not only lacked personal awareness, they also lacked social awareness. They were unable to read the interpersonal signs of others and events in their social context. They were described as insensitive to others and, in some cases, even arrogant. They were not able to respond appropriately to interpersonal relations and some were seen as bullying, aloof, untrustworthy or micro-managers. Basically they did not know how to manage relationships effectively. Further studies that continued into the 2000s found much the same thing.[7]

Major factors contributing to derailment

The highlight from two decades of research into executive derailment is that derailment is usually associated with a lack of interpersonal skills, poor engagement of the team, a failure to manage context and general hubris.

Lack of interpersonal skills

Poor interpersonal skills topped the list of flaws: they pretty much always do. I know a senior doctor whose technical skills I would want in any medical emergency. However, his lack of eye contact, nervous shuffling, abrupt silences and conversations that do not connect make small talk very difficult. He wouldn't be my first choice as a travelling companion. His fellow executive directors described him as aloof and arrogant. He knew how they felt and

---

[7] McCall, Jnr, M.W. (1999), *High Flyers: Developing the Next Generation of Leaders*, Harvard Business School Press, Boston, Mass.

wanted to have contact, but found it difficult to change. So he remained in his own technical world.

Poor team engagement

A failure to manage your team was a close second. It is hard enough to keep good team spirit. During periods of change and working virtually the pressures are even more pressing. A study on transformational CEOs by a team of researchers showed that their effectiveness would be moderated – increased or decreased – by the congruency and alignment of their executive team.[8]

Failure to manage the context

The other common theme across the studies is the lack of networking and political skills. The problem is typically a failure to manage the context. In earlier studies, it tended to be a failure to manage the boss.

EXAMPLE

Failure to manage the bosses

Martin Jones managed a country office in Europe for an American consulting firm. It was a new territory for the firm but he really fitted the required profile. He was independently minded, experienced at running smaller firms, knew the market and had fresh ideas on growing the business and restructuring the business model. But all the reporting requirements, both to Europe and the United States, frustrated him. Decisions from head office were slow. The European practice leader appeared interfering rather than aiding the new ideas. As an experienced hire, he began to resent the seeming control from both his immediate boss and the US parent. It didn't take long for misunderstandings to escalate. Misinformation reinforced poor relations. A problem of differences turned chronic. After nearly two years things reached rock bottom. Martin and his boss fell out and before long he was hiring lawyers to negotiate his leaving package. His career in the company came to an untimely end. He had derailed owing to a failure to manage his bosses in Europe and the United States.

---

[8] Colbert, A.E., Kristof-Brown, A.L., Bradley, B.H. and Smith, M.R. (2008) 'CEO Transformational Leadership: The Role of Goal Importance Congruence in Top Management Teams', *Academy of Management Journal*, 51, 1, pp.81–96.

More broadly, the issue is now about managing the context and, particularly, the political context. Fred Luthans, a senior professor in organisational behaviour from Nabraska University, undertook a four-year observational study of what managers actually do.[9] His study looked at over 300 managers and his results were surprising. He found that there were two types of executives:

1 Successful executives navigated the demands of organisational life. They were promoted very quickly.

2 Effective executives tended to do the job to high standards and within resource constraints. However, they tended not to gain traction on the corporate ladder.

What made the difference? The single most important variable that made a difference was the extent of social networking. Successful managers tended to engage in more communication, social interaction and organisational politiking. The message is clear. It is not enough to do a good job. You also need to be good at managing stakeholders and networks. It doesn't make it right, of course, but that is how it is. Politics can seem an unsavoury activity, but it is a fact of organisational life. Building social capital (discussed in Chapter 7) creates leverage for change as relationships act as powerful tools for engagement.

So, ask yourself: Do you know who your main stakeholders are in the organisation? Who are the people who can influence your fortunes? Who do you need to keep informed? It is worth thinking how often – if ever – you undertake stakeholder analysis? Things and people change so I usually recommend clients to refresh their analysis on a regular basis.

Change requires you to manage your constituencies, stakeholders and powerful influences in your network of associates. The risk is derailment or being passed over. On the positive side, it means you are anticipating and actively responding to the naturally conflicting interests of different groups. Remember that a plurality of differences was the basis of ancient democracy and forms part of the human

[9] Luthans, F. (1988), 'Successful vs. Effective Real Managers', *Academy of Management Executive*, 11, 2, pp.127–32.

condition. Politics does not have to be a dirty word. In fact without it organisations would be even more difficult to manage.

General hubris

Hubris is the final catch-all and trip wire of derailment.[10] It can be a combination of a lack of self-awareness, over-confidence and reliance on past glory or success with thinking that the expertise that got you to where you are will continue into the future. In Greek mythology, the term means excessive pride or arrogance. It evokes a punishing response from the gods and becomes the fatal flaw. In organisational life, it can lead to a loss of status at one end or your job at the other.

> Managers can increase their emotional and social intelligence to be more effective in interpersonal relations and management of social networks.

Fit or misfit?

Successful leaders build internal capability. In the same way this is important for the organisation, it is also true for leaders of change.

Earlier, I listed the main characteristics of effective advocates of change, but these also have to operate in an organisational context. As we have seen, organisations that are ready for change will provide a better base for leading change. As a result, effective personal readiness and organisational readiness are both required to make the most of the opportunities for change. The final question must be whether there is a fit between your personal mastery and the state of your organisation's readiness.

We know that people go through transitions. It can take months and we can feel doubt and worry. These feelings are natural. I think of how many times I have heard highly paid and successful executives question if they are good enough. They have a sense that they may be found out and exposed as a fraud. We also know that these feelings of transition will be affected by personal predilections and the organisational context.

[10] See an interesting read on hubris by Strebel, P. and Ohlsson, A.-V. (2008) *Smart Big Moves*, FT Prentice Hall, London.

The lessons from this book and your SCi results give you an indication of your organisation's readiness. You can squarely answer the question: Does this company or department have changeability?

But, can you answer the same question for yourself? You have reviewed the characteristics of an effective change leader. You have read other people's stories on being both successful and unsuccessful. On a scale of 1 to 10, what is your personal changeability rating? How ready do you think you are as a change leader? Depending on your response, you have some personal strategies that complement your organisational change strategies.[11]

Assessing your organisational readiness and your own provides a helpful map for adopting personal strategies – see Figure 12.1.

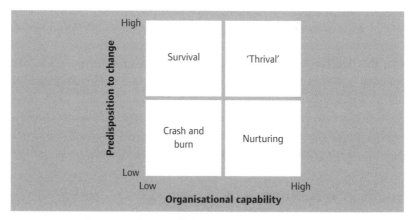

FIGURE 12.1 A personal map of change

I see executives faced with four main scenarios.

Scenario 1: Crash and burn

You do not want to start here. It is an unstable cocktail of those that have a low tolerance or disposition to change and operate within an organisation that also has poor readiness. These conditions form the recipe for potential danger. The experience for those in this situation is difficult. They would prefer things to stay the same. They want

[11] Take time to review your action plan in Appendix 3.

certainty. They prefer continuity. A director in one of the mono-line insurance companies knew intuitively something was not right. The markets were changing but his company was not. He was fearful of what he read in the papers and began to fret constantly about his team and business. This continued until he was relieved of duty because of a stress-related illness. But it was a self-fulfilling prophecy. It does not always have to end this way.

What can you do?

Operating in this scenario is the most difficult. It is like being dragged through wild bushes by a horse competing for first place at the Derby. The challenge for you is to develop a sense of personal confidence, resilience and authority. For some the answer is reframing the situation. One executive was able to see things from a different perspective. While the changes were threatening, he was able to gain recognition for his area of technical specialism in a way that was previously ignored. This made a significant difference to his contribution. Others find that making behavioural changes can help or that they have the choice to step away and do something differently. In a situation where it's making you unhappy, creating chronic stress and causing illness, I warn you not to come to me for coaching. I will definitely recommend you walk from any situation that's so bad. Life is too short.

Scenario 2: Survival

This is a situation when there is personal willingness to entertain and lead change, but you operate in an organisation that has poor readiness and does not have a clue about managing transitions. The goal is personal survival, regroup and find where you might make some headway. In December 2007, I received a call from an organisational effectiveness specialist working in a bank involved in a merger and acquisition. She felt that nobody really knew what they were doing, the company was losing value as programme management had not touched the cultural aspects of either of the companies and the benefits of the merger were going to be lost. Here is a change specialist in survival mode. Afterwards, I realised the purpose of the call wasn't really to get advice or get a solution.

She wanted someone to talk it through with and get a sanity check. Sound familiar?

What can you do?

Managers need social and organisational support. They have the personal authority to make a difference but are working in a chaotic or unsatisfactory situation. Here emotional resilience has to be matched with social networks. The best options are to use your network of friends and colleagues for support. Use a mentor or executive coach. Use the political networks in the organisation. Gain buy-in to pilot projects that fall within your area of responsibility and make sure you have cover from the top by a senior sponsor.

Scenario 3: Nurturing

The table turns slightly in your favour. The organisation is ready but you are not. These organisations form islands of peace. Good companies that are ready for change anticipate such situations as part of the process. They see fear and uncertainty as natural and understand that change is very personal. Each person has a different experience. They will help those less ready to change to engage intellectually and emotionally and guide them through the process of organisational change. They also help those that need to move on to leave with dignity.

What can you do?

Where you are less confident but operate in an organisation that is ready for change, there is a temporary reprieve. There is a chance to use the time to get ready yourself. Ask questions about the changes. Become informed about the things that are to be different. Get rid of the doubts and get answers to what's in it for me!

Joe was uncertain about what would happen in his new role in the IT Group, when the reorganisation was announced. Between you and me, he was petrified. However, he asked his new boss what the score was. He gathered from mature discussions that he probably had a job for two years. He wasn't happy about the news but knew what the deal was for the next two years. I saw him after the dust had settled and he was entertaining thoughts of moving abroad and retiring early. A small piece of information put his mind at ease. For some, it might not work. But for Joe, his boss and the organisation, this solution worked.

Scenario 4: 'Thrival'

The final scenario refers to those people who work in organisations that are ready for change and are also ready themselves. They tend to set the pace for change. Their behaviours are reinforced by their colleagues, bosses and the organisation's culture. 'The fit between people's preferences and organisations' cultures tend to be positively correlated.'[12] In some companies they make sure there is fit through the recruitment process, then take you through induction (or indoctrination) and finally promote people on the same basis. In high-performance cultures, they may reinforce this with a two-year up or out policy. Where companies score high on readiness to change and have people who are positively predisposed to change then, this makes for a win-win situation.

What can you do?

The signs are positive in these organisations. There is an opportunity to make change a reality. But remember the ones you leave behind. Lack of sensitivity to those who are not like you is often the problem. Executives may not realise that they can form in-groups and out-groups unintentionally. You can sometimes see it in their 360-degree feedback where there is a split across their direct reports. Gentle enquiry usually reveals that managers tend to give work, feedback and opportunities to people like themselves. They do not realise that have just alienated half the team and lost their goodwill and traction. Hopefully, if they are an effective change leader, then this can be avoided.

[12] Chatman, J. (1991) 'Matching People and Organisations: Selection and Socializing in Public Accounting Firms', *Administrative Quarterly Review*, 36, pp.459–84 and O'Reilly III, C.A., Chatman, J. and Caldwell, D.F. (1991) 'People and Organizational Culture: A Profile Comparison Approach to Assessing Person-Organization Fit', *Academy of Management Journal*, 34, 3, pp.487–516.

Thus, your personal journey will be heightened or dampened by your predisposition, and the organisation's readiness for change.

Managers can be more skilful in managing their own journey

Align with the change agenda

The story of this book is that successful change requires alignment of the external world, the internal capabilities and readiness of the organisation, and the leadership style of the change advocate: *changeability*. Most of the time wasted in change and the high failure rate is due to this misalignment.

Do all three fit for your situation? When it works well, change delivers results. Apple's Steve Jobs displays many qualities of an effective change leader. We saw some of these demonstrated in Chapter 11. But there are four qualities that have been particularly noted.[13]

Steve Jobs illustrates leadership qualities. He knows his people and the business. He matured with his industry and was intimately involved in the company in its early days. The Centre of Creative Leadership suggests this is a critical predictor of leadership success.

'Look, I was very luck to have grown up with this industry. I did everything in the early days – documentation, sales, supply chain, sweeping the floors, buying chips – you name it. I put computers together with my own two hands. And as the industry grew up, I kept on doing it,' says Jobs.[14] This deep knowledge allows him to see the future of the industry, anticipate trends and develop products to meet future needs.

Tuned into the industry context, Jobs can move quickly – even when things go wrong. When Apple slashed prices just two months after launching its iPhone, customers who had paid full price were outraged. Jobs quickly admitted the company's mistake in an open letter to customers and offered $100 credit in Apple stores for those buying at the original prices.

[13] Barrile, S. (2006) 'Ingredients for the success of the Apple iPod: innovation', *Businessdate*, July, 14, 3, pp.5–7.

[14] Extract from an interview with Steve Jobs, *Business Week Online,* 4 October 2004.

Jobs also sets clear goals and priorities. He was clear when the iMac was designed what he wanted. In 2001, he set clear targets for management to create a ground-breaking music player that resulted in the iPod. He is demanding but passionate. It is an approach that creates a sense of followership rather than fear.

He follows through on his commitments. His drive for perfection and results can bring out the autocratic side of his management style. Yet Jobs is able to balance this with a consultative style when required. Most leaders have a preferred style of management. Flexing one's style is an important element – particularly in a changing environment. Otherwise, make sure you have a good team. Jobs understands the importance of recruiting the right people.

An additional ingredient in Steve Jobs's change armoury is that he knows himself. Strength of character is important. So is being honest with yourself – about your strengths and weaknesses. He seems to score well on these. He dealt well with being forced out of his own company in 1985, developing NeXT and Pixar during his years in the wilderness. He returned to Apple without rancour. He has drawn very personal lessons from his diagnosis in 2004 of pancreatic cancer. His counsel to Stanford University graduates at a public address was: 'Your time is limited, so don't waste it living someone else's life... Don't let the noise of others' opinions drown out your own inner voice.'

Jobs has many of the qualities of a transformational leader. I think this form of leadership is for those in the Zen zone. However, we saw very clearly in Part 3 that strategies for change need different types of leadership depending on the external conditions and the internal capabilities of the company.

We also saw that transactional leadership and a steady pair of hands on the tiller suited the steady state zone (Chapter 8). This was illustrated in the case of Peter, who worked tirelessly as the turnaround leader. Similarly Terry Dial and Ron Whatford in Chapter 9 had a turnaround strategy for the retail banking arm of Lloyds TSB. Finally, the visionary or disruptive leadership style tends to suit the complacent comfort zone (see Chapter 10). The goal being to shake up the dominant logic that leads to lower performance and challenges prevalent and often implicit assumptions.

When I want to use shock tactics with a client or students, I will say: the only thing that stops change in this organisation is the people in this room. They are outraged and protest. But soon enough, after thoughtful dialogue, they get it. Change is as much about them as it is about the organisation.

Personal mastery means managing yourself, managing your relationships, managing your context and gaining alignment on all fronts. Navigating these competing demands is one of the secrets of being an effective leader of change.

Summary

▌ The qualities of a successful change agent mirror those of a successful company.

▌ Personal change does not happen simply by thinking about it. Conviction, courage and capability are critical for the head, heart and hands.

▌ Leading change requires you to have a clear and sophisticated understanding of your organisation and to guard against derailment.

▌ You need to have a personal routine that builds your own development and personal capabilities – emotional intelligence, political intelligence and social intelligence.

▌ There are times when you and the company are aligned and times when you are not. Alignment is essential. Knowing when you are not in sync is half the battle. Doing something about it is the other. Clear strategies to change then follow, depending on the results of your organisational and personal assessments.

▌ You always have choices – internally you can decide to let go and think about what's working, and externally you can always make a difference. Remember, the final choice is always yours.

Epilogue: Back to base

'There is nothing so useful as a theory.'

Kurt Lewin

As an academic, I love a good theory. We progress by standing on the shoulders of others. Thus, I have drawn on a wide range of rigorous research that has laid the foundations for the key concepts and ideas in this book. The efforts of hundreds of researchers and academics informed my research questions and methodologies.

However, theory on its own does not help managers improve their practice, deliver their goods and services with greater effectiveness or necessarily make them feel more confident. Most want to make a difference to their own lives and those of the people around them.

The purpose of this book is to provide readers with a fast route to the enduring theories, concepts and research in the field of organisational behaviour and link these with cases, personal experiences and tips on what you might do as a manager. It does not claim to be comprehensive and it's impossible to put everything into one book. You have a map, clearly charted waters, a sense of your boat's capabilities, the qualities of an effective helmsman (or woman) and know what you need to do for alignment. You also have the experiences and lessons from others.

So what next? What are you going to do about it? At the end of a class or workshop, I like to ask three questions. I call it my 3–2–1. I am going to ask you the same:

1 What three things did you learn? The ones that really stand out. You may have a fresh insight, a different perspective on an old problem or you may be reminded of things that were lost in the slumber of routine – implicit knowledge. What were they?

2 What two things are you taking back into the business? These are things you take back and try to implement or experiment with. What resources might you need? Who will you need to get on board with the idea? How might you engage them?

3 What one thing are you going to do on Monday? What will you actually do as an initial step to making a difference? The first step is often the most difficult but it does not have to be radical.

So before you close this book, reflect now: What are your 3–2–1 from the book? Jot them down and revisit them on a monthly basis.

Changing the odds

There are some clear themes that run through each part of this book that make a difference. If you take nothing else away from the book, remember these key points.

Why change?

A crisis helps. But that's probably not the way you want to start. We discovered that the demands of the environment matter. These dependencies are the key drivers of change. They may be the result of a change in demographics or disruptive technology. They can put a market leader such as Polaroid very quickly in the 'change avoider' category without it even realising that this has happened. Companies that detect, anticipate and embrace change see the external turbulence as an opportunity as well as a challenge.

What needs changing?

The answer to this question is: it depends. Are you trying to develop a new market segment; align the structures of two recently merged companies; or get better at doing what you already do? We know that the change agenda follows the strategic agenda and a poor strategy or poorly communicated one will undermine your efforts. But strategy on its own is not enough. Implementation makes the difference. You need changeability.

Change is ever-present and can be difficult. Incremental change for one company can be a tsunami for another. The key point is to understand the nature, size and scope of the change and be clear about why you are doing it and what problem you are trying to solve. A relentless focus is critical for success as the stumbling blocks make us easy prey for failure. Once you are clear on your goals for change then what makes a difference is your readiness.

The organisations that successfully navigate the waves of change have great internal capabilities:

▌ They constantly scan the environment.

▌ They draw insightful meanings from their detections.

▌ They collaborate and innovate internally.

▌ They do not let politics and petty differences get in the way.

▌ They deliver through structures that enable fluid execution.

You may remember the examples of Apple, Google, Toyota and P&G and how they featured these distinct qualities. You need to join this startlingly select group.

We also see that there are further benefits. Those individuals and organisations that change seem to find it easier the next time and so build a core competency in the process of change. Over time, this increasingly becomes a source of competitive advantage. Thus, change becomes an exciting venture, rather than something to be feared.

How to change?

Strategies for change depend on alignment. The additional insight was that the external environment tends to favour change strategies depending on your organisation's internal capabilities. Part 3 addressed these in detail:

▌ Keep trim and go for incremental changes in steady state zones.

▌ Turnaround with radical restructuring when operating in a turbulent environment. Do it quickly and have clear priorities.

▌ De-conform – disrupt and challenge the dominant norms and logic. Get energised. Mobilise for change if you are operating in the comfort zone

▌ Ride the waves of change – expect the changes before they arrive. Lead the changes if there's a lag when in the Zen zone.

Leadership holds it together

Leadership makes a difference. Indeed, it is the job of a leader to make a difference. The transformational leader is still alive and a critical part of the change agenda. Allen Leighton, Richard Ward, Anne Mulcahy and many others were the key driving forces for change in their organisations. You do not have to be one of these characters. As my colleagues Rob Goffee and Gareth Jones at London Business School point out, there is only one Jack Welch so why try and copy him? The intelligent response is to adapt the style that suits your context and personal style.

▌ Transactional leadership operates best in the steady state. They do things right, focus on short-term goals and incremental changes.

▌ Turnaround change agents rip up the old and drive through the necessary changes, often for organisational survival. This has a short life but provides you with a crucial kick-start if faced with these circumstances.

▌ Visionary leaders provide an image of the future that is not easily understood now. They can paint a vivid picture of how great it could be or a doomsday scenario to get people out of the comfort zone.

▌ Transformational change leaders galvanise people's hearts, minds and hands to make changes in a timely and constant fashion.

The styles may overlap or blur at the edges. But they provide clarity of direction and must be used with flexibility as circumstances change.

Remember the leader's effectiveness can be moderated by the environment as well as by their executive team. The research tells us this but again we saw the same effect with leaders that draw upon an inner team that help make change happen. It certainly made the difference for Xerox, Pepsi-Co, Microsoft and the changes at Asda, all mentioned earlier.

Stakeholder engagement completes the picture. We saw how many companies devised a variety of engagement strategies in order to get buy-in. This activity takes up the most time, outcomes are vague and results unpredictable. But notice how often change initiatives deployed it. It took several forms. Individual leaders would visit local branches or sites and talk to the troops. Others ran workshops and got people to contribute. Again, another method was through cross-functional task teams. It matters not so much about the detail. But the principle marks the difference between companies. So mobilise the workforce.

Is change here to stay?

I am literally writing this final piece on the train having run a very enjoyable workshop with an agency that specialises in environmental issues. In the last exercise, participants were asked to imagine a world in 2040. The result was a curious mix. One said we'd have a half world: with fewer people, most of the planet under water, no children. Space would be at even more of a premium and we would be operating on nuclear fuels with most of the waste exported to another galaxy.

Another talked of a scenario where Earth plc had managed to stop and reverse the planet's decline. Some ice caps remained, sea levels were beginning to fall and sustainable developments were forming part of the answer.

The other two scenarios were more optimistic. The planet was safe. We had gone back to smaller communities. Small scale production was the norm. Technology and the natural elements – wind, water and the sun – met all our energy needs. It was a beautiful world.

The point is not that one is right or the other wrong. The key point is that we will always need to change:

▌ Demographic changes mean we will have larger and older populations that will affect lifestyles, the distribution of income and market spending power.

▌ Technology continues to advance: neurogenesis and nano-technology combines; biotech solutions to ageing; increased brainpower and body implants. Imagine we might become walking robots.

▌ Financial crises will follow long-run Kondratiev waves lasting 50 years as well as 10-year business cycles. The world is getting richer but the ups and downs may be more extreme and questions of distribution remain.

▌ Social and geo-political dynamics continue. There are conflicts in every part of the world which create unstable conditions for societies and economies. These will force changes.

▌ Oil prices hit a peak of $147.27 in the third quarter of 2008. They doubled from 2007 prices. Goldman Sachs was forecasting $200 a barrel at the time of writing. They are a long way from the oil companies' fears at the end of 1990s of $10 a barrel. It'll be interesting to see what the prices are by the time you get to this page. You will probably be looking at these numbers with disbelief.

There will always be change driven from external factors in our complex and ever-changing world. Thus, organisations and their leaders will always need to respond.

Navigating the last leg

It is fitting to end how we started, on the water with another family sailing story. Setting out on a journey is always exciting. Returning brings its own rewards: a sense of achievement, respite, relief and a time to rest. The anticipation is palpable. Such was the case a few years ago on another memorable family sailing day in Salcombe Bay. We'd had perfect weather and sailed from one beach to another. Starting at East Portlemouth, we moved on to Mill Bay, ending with a picnic on South Sands.

The afternoon sun was beginning to fall and it was about six in the evening. We'd dropped off the main party, and a small crew of my middle son, a novice sailing friend – Auntie Mary – and myself made our way back to our mooring. It was bliss – a perfect way to end a perfect day.

Our novice passenger enquired, 'What are you doing?' I explained the wind was gently blowing behind us and between my son on the jib and myself we were on a run – wind coming from behind the stern. One could imagine the trade winds taking spices and treats between Europe and the Americas in much the same way with large sails billowing in the wind. I think the sound of the water and a sense of peace led me to the next action. 'Would you like to have a try?' I asked.

I'm not sure what I expected her to say. Perhaps, I thought she would decline. But Auntie Mary picked up the challenge with gusto and before I knew it had planted herself squarely at the helm with hand on tiller. Here was a woman who was prepared to try something new, something fresh and exciting. It was great. The wind slowly picked up and I felt a slight surge in our vessel. 'Are you all right?' I asked as the wind pulled at the sails. 'No problem,' was the reply. 'What happens if I push the tiller away?' 'Don't do …' but my sentence was never completed.

The boat began to roll and the boom swung over with the force of a sledge hammer. For the technical among you, this manoeuvre of a gybing can be tricky even for a practised sailor. With a novice at the helm and unexpected swing, the inevitability of our situation soon became apparent. As if in slow motion, I felt my balance going, the boat heeling to the side and the lower part of my body becoming damp.

The next few moments were a blur. The whole boat tipped over, we were submerged in the cold waters of the bay, completely capsized! What a way to end the day.

Emerging from the clutches of a cold sea, I looked around for the crew. Within moments, both my son and I knew exactly what to do. Stay connected with the boat. See if we can right her. Stay calm. The real hero of the moment was my son who followed out the routine to the letter. In fact, he was the one saying to Auntie Mary, 'Don't worry, we'll be fine.' It didn't take long before our 'accident' had attracted much interest, humour and a little sympathetic concern. The local coast master ensured our safety and the rescue was routine. We righted the boat, took her into the mooring while bailing out the excess water. The day ended unexpectedly cold and wet.

Change is around us all the time. On this occasion the outcome was a cold, wet surprise. But, happily, we were ready even for that. We were prepared for the unexpected. We were wearing life jackets. The capsize routines we'd practised over and over again, the clarity of roles, the sense of seeing it as a challenge rather than fearfully, made us ready for change. Even though it wasn't what we hoped for, we were able to cope – and to laugh about it afterwards. More than that, we came through the test with flying colours, and were stronger for it.

Change comes in many guises. It happens whether you want it or not. What makes all the difference is how you respond – whether you as a person, and as a leader, are ready to face the challenge. So I will finish with a simple question: Do you have changeability – organisationally and personally – and are you prepared to do what it takes to get there? My hope is that after reading this book, you will.

Bon voyage and good luck.

Appendix 1: Research note

We wanted to know what makes the difference between success and failure in navigating change. The research ran over a period of six years and used an iteration of 12 in-depth case studies to get qualitative depth and a pragmatic approach alongside a wider survey to gain greater generality. It started with a pilot group of case studies to test out the dominant theories before then administering the wider survey.

A 90-item questionnaire was designed and tested for sense using a Q-Sort methodology and we gained an inter-rater reliability of 0.75. The questionnaire was also tested for its internal consistency, construct validity and scale validity. These tests were fully met. The statistical procedure of exploratory factor analysis was used to identify the underlying principle and independent components that helped to explain the essentials of successful change.

We surveyed some 5,000 managers from 255 business units. This cross-sectional study had a sample of international companies' business units mainly operating in Europe but covering countries as diverse as Australia and Zimbabwe. The companies represented financial services organisations, pharmaceutical and health care organisations, transport, manufacturing and natural resources. There were also a number of public-sector organisations.

We achieved a response rate of 55 per cent. These were taken from middle management (48 per cent), senior management (33 per cent), top management (CEO, CFO, MD) (7 per cent), with the remaining respondents (12 per cent) being professional roles or other categories.

The number of people within each unit that responded ranged from 8 to 169 respondents and this was a function of the size and scope of the individual business unit as well as the organisation's structure.

The five factors were the result of a two-stage factor analysis: first using an exploratory approach then a confirmatory factor analysis to test our hypothesis and determine best fit. Items that loaded with a factor >0.4 with no cross loading of >0.3 were included. Each factor result positively correlated to questions on successful change:

▌ Organisational scanning routines (0.50)

▌ Top teams that were insightful (0.71)

▌ Open and innovative cultures (0.71)

▌ Functional routines (0.60)

▌ Cohesive organisational structures (0.62).

The overall score of each business unit's change capability was normed, using a sten score, to make like-for-like comparisons. It suggested three statistically significant types of change capabilities varying from low (one standard deviation below the mean), average and high (one standard deviation) from the mean.

These differences in profile also took into account the environmental conditions. Using an ANOVA statistical test we determined there was statistically significant difference between high, medium and low capability organisations operating in the same environment (from volatile to stable) and profit trends. Respondents reported that high-change-capability organisations reported more positive trends in profits than their lower-change counterparts.

However, as the environment became more stable, the influence of the organisation's change capability lessened so that in a more stable external environment there were no significant differences between high-, medium- and low-change-capability organisations.

Appendix 2: Does your organisation have changeability?

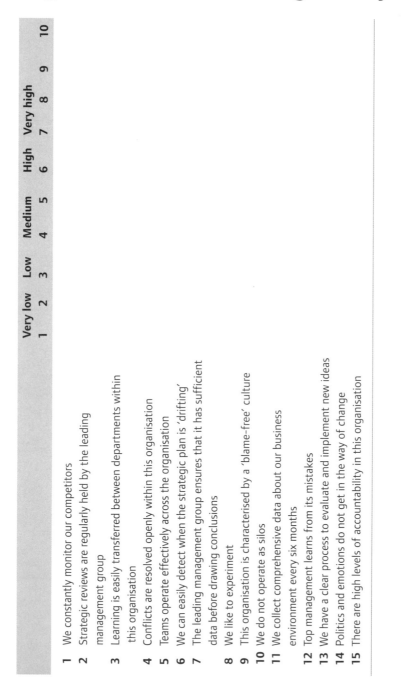

	Very low	Low	Medium	High	Very high	
	1	2	3	4	5	6	7	8	9	10

1 We constantly monitor our competitors

2 Strategic reviews are regularly held by the leading management group

3 Learning is easily transferred between departments within this organisation

4 Conflicts are resolved openly within this organisation

5 Teams operate effectively across the organisation

6 We can easily detect when the strategic plan is 'drifting'

7 The leading management group ensures that it has sufficient data before drawing conclusions

8 We like to experiment

9 This organisation is characterised by a 'blame-free' culture

10 We do not operate as silos

11 We collect comprehensive data about our business environment every six months

12 Top management learns from its mistakes

13 We have a clear process to evaluate and implement new ideas

14 Politics and emotions do not get in the way of change

15 There are high levels of accountability in this organisation

Find out by completing the questionnaire.

The full version of the SCi Strategic Capability Questionnaire is available by going to the Ilyas Jarrett website at: www.ilyasjarrett.com.

Understanding your results

Scoring

Add up your answer for each of the following questions:

▌ Scanning (Q1 + 6 + 11)   =

▌ Reading (Q2 + 7 + 12)   =

▌ Harnessing (Q3 + 8 +13)   =

▌ Weighing (Q4 + 9 + 14)   =

▌ Execution (Q5 + 10 + 15)   =

Total score   =

Divide the total by 5 to get the **final score** =

Interpreting your score

For each factor

▌ Scores 1–9:   Needs considerable development

▌ Scores 10–23: Room for improvement (average score is 15)

▌ Scores 24–30: A capability strength – maintain trim

Overall strategic capability = Average of all factors

Appendix 3: What is the nature of your environment?

Environmental volatility questionnaire

	Strongly disagree	Disagree	Somewhat agree	Agree	Strongly agree
1 There are more than six key competitors in our market	1	2	3	4	5
2 Competitors are constantly entering and leaving the market	1	2	3	4	5
3 There are continual innovations and technological advancements in the industry	1	2	3	4	5
4 Clients/customers' needs are constantly changing	1	2	3	4	5
5 It is easy to differentiate our products/services	1	2	3	4	5
6 Competition can come from substitutes to our products/ services readily available outside of the core industry	1	2	3	4	5
7 Our industry is experiencing low growth – less than 2 per cent per annum	1	2	3	4	5
8 The political system in the country in which we operate is unstable	1	2	3	4	5
9 Our industry is not highly regulated	1	2	3	4	5
10 Our industry is under public scrutiny from ethical or environmental perspectives	1	2	3	4	5

Total _____

The full version of the SCi Strategic Capability Questionnaire is available by going to the Ilyas Jarrett website www.ilyasjarrett.com

Interpreting your score

Environment

▌ Scores 10–20 suggest a relatively stable environment

▌ Scores 21–40 suggest medium-paced changes in the environment

▌ Scores 41–50 suggest a fast-paced and increasingly volatile environment

Appendix 4: Personal action plan

Once you have ascertained the key areas in which you need to build personal capabilities, the next step is doing something about it.

Step 1: Review your areas for action

HEAD

HEART

HANDS

Step 2: Considering the points you have listed in all three areas, prioritise 3–5 overall to concentrate on high impact, low effort as the first ones to achieve

Step 3: Identify next steps for action

Development goal	Activities (describe key activities – be as specific as possible)	Resources/support needed	By when

Step 4: Prepare for a one-to-one session with your executive coach

Key notes/points

Step 5: Please review your actions on:

Time	Date	Notes (please attach separate sheets for further notes)
4 weeks	w/b	
3 months	w/b	
Another session		
6–12 months	w/b	

Appendix 5

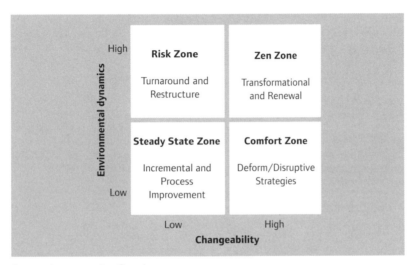

Dynamic strategies for change

Index